Confucianism

Titles in the Religions of the World series include:

- Buddhism
- Confucianism
- Hinduism
- Islam
- Shinto

Confucianism

Louise Chipley Slavicek

Lucent Books, Inc.
10911 Technology Place, San Diego, California 92127

For my mother, Julie W. Chipley

Library of Congress Cataloging-in-Publication Data

Slavicek, Louise Chipley, 1956–
Confucianism / By Louise Chipley Slavicek.
p. cm. — (Religions of the world)
Summary : Discusses what Confucianism is, the life, times, and teachings of Confucius, and the spread and practice of Confucianism in modern times.
ISBN 1-5006-984-8 (alk. paper)
1. Confucianism—Juvenile literature. 2. Confucius—Juvenile literature. [1. Confucianism. 2. Confucius.] I. Title. II Religions of the world (Lucent Books)
BL1853 .S55 2002
181' . 112—dc21

2001005773

an imprint of the Gale Group
10911 Technology Place, San Diego, California 92127

Printed in the U.S.A.

Contents

Foreword		6
Introduction	What Is Confucianism?	8
Chapter 1	Confucius: His Life and Times: 551 B.C.–479 B.C.	11
Chapter 2	Confucianism Emerges: The Fifth Through the Third Centuries B.C.	28
Chapter 3	The Changing Fortunes of Confucianism in China: The Qin Through the Tang Dynasties: 221 B.C.–A.D. 960	45
Chapter 4	The Apex of Confucianism: Confucianism in China and East Asia from the Tenth to the Twentieth Centuries	62
Chapter 5	From Vilification to Rehabilitation: Confucianism in Twentieth-Century China	81
Chapter 6	The Relevance of Confucianism Today	98
Appendix: The Pinyin System		113
Notes		114
Glossary		117
For Further Reading		119
Works Consulted		120
Index		123
Picture Credits		128
About the Author		128

Foreword

Religion has always been a central component of human culture, though its form and practice have changed through time. Ancient people lived in a world they could not explain or comprehend. Their world consisted of an environment controlled by vague and mysterious powers attributed to a wide array of gods. Artifacts dating to a time before recorded history suggest that the religion of the distant past reflected this world, consisting mainly of rituals devised to influence events under the control of these gods.

The steady advancement of human societies brought about changes in religion as in all other things. Through time, religion came to be seen as a system of beliefs and practices that gave meaning to—or allowed acceptance of—anything that transcended the natural or the known. And, the belief in many gods ultimately was replaced in many cultures by the belief in a Supreme Being.

As in the distant past, however, religion still provides answers to timeless questions: How, why, and by whom was the universe created? What is the ultimate meaning of human life? Why is life inevitably followed by death? Does the human soul continue to exist after death, and if so, in what form? Why is there pain and suffering in the world, and why is there evil?

In addition, all the major world religions provide their followers with a concrete and clearly stated ethical code. They offer a set of moral instructions, defining virtue and evil and what is required to achieve goodness. One of these universal moral codes is compassion toward others above all else. Thus, Judaism, Christianity, Islam, Hinduism, Buddhism, Confucianism, and Taoism each teach a version of the so-called golden rule, or in the words of Jesus Christ, "As ye would that men should do to you, do ye also to them likewise." (Luke 6:31) For example, Confucius instructed his disciples to "never impose on others what you would not choose for yourself." (*Analects*: 12:2) The Hindu epic poem, *Mahabarata*, identifies the core of all Hindu teaching as not doing unto others what you do not wish done to yourself, and Muhammad declared that no Muslim could be a true believer unless he desired for his brother no less than that which he desires for himself.

It is ironic, then, that although compassionate concern for others forms the heart of all the major religions' moral teachings, religion has also been at the root of countless conflicts throughout history. It has been suggested that much of the appeal that religions hold for humankind lies in their unswerving faith in the truth of their particular vision. Throughout history, most religions have shared a profound confidence that their interpretation of life, God, and the universe is the right one, thus giving their followers a sense of certainty in an uncertain and often fragile existence. Given the assurance displayed by most religions regarding the fundamental correctness of their teachings and practices, it is perhaps not surprising that religious intolerance has fueled disputes and even full-scale wars between peoples and nations time and time again, from the Crusades of medieval times to the current bloodshed in Northern Ireland and the Middle East.

Today, as violent religious conflicts trouble many parts of our world, it has become more important than ever to learn about the similarities as well as the differences between faiths. One of the most effective ways to accomplish this is by examining the beliefs, customs, and values of various religions. In the Lucent Books Religions of the World series, students will find a clear description of the core creeds, rituals, ethical teachings, and sacred texts of the world's major religions. In-depth explorations of how these faiths changed over time, how they have influenced the social customs, laws, and education of the countries in which they are practiced, and the particular challenges each one faces in coming years are also featured.

Extensive quotations from primary source materials, especially the core scriptures of each faith, and a generous number of secondary source quotations from the works of respected modern scholars are included in each volume in the series. It is hoped that by gaining insight into the faiths of other peoples and nations, students will not only gain a deeper appreciation and respect for different religious beliefs and practices, but will also gain new perspectives on and understanding of their own religious traditions.

introduction

What Is Confucianism?

The system of thought known as Confucianism has its roots in the teachings of the Chinese scholar Confucius, who lived about twenty-five hundred years ago. Confucius devised a set of guidelines for individual moral development and for creating a harmonious, orderly society. After his death, his disciples collected and preserved his ideas, which later thinkers refined and expanded. For many years, Confucianism competed for the approval of the Chinese people and leadership with a host of other philosophies. Finally, under the Han dynasty which ruled China from about 200 B.C. to A.D. 200, Confucianism won the backing of the Chinese government. By the beginning of Christianity, Confucianism had become China's official ideology and the central focus of its educational system. As Confucianism gained more and more influence over Chinese political, intellectual, and social life, it also spread to other East Asian countries, particularly Korea, Japan, and Vietnam.

During the late nineteenth and early twentieth centuries, Confucianism lost its dominant position in the political and educational systems of China and other East Asian countries. Yet, throughout the modern era, the moral teachings that form the heart of Confucianism have continued to mold the attitudes and behavior of millions of people in East Asia and in Chinese communities around the globe

Layered roofs cover a fourteenth-century Confucian temple in Beijing, China.

from San Francisco to London to Melbourne. It is impossible to determine the exact number of Confucians worldwide today, for Confucianism has no formal church or other organized body that can be statistically analyzed. The *World Almanac* states that there were at least 6 million Confucians in East Asia and elsewhere in the world at the end of the twentieth century. Yet this number is almost certainly far too low. For in East Asia, where most Confucians reside, many people may identify themselves as Daoists, Buddhists, Shintoists, or members of other religious faiths, but are still followers of Confucius. In contrast to the West, in East Asia religions are typically neither exclusive nor competitive. Thus, a person might observe Confucian rules of morality and decorum, yet call on a Daoist priest for assistance in times of illness, or worship occasionally at a Buddhist temple, all without feeling that he or she had been untrue to any of the three different traditions.

Confucianism: Religion or Philosophy?

If uncertainty surrounds the issue of how many Confucians there are in the world today, an even more fundamental question regarding Confucianism has deeply divided contemporary scholars: Is Confucianism a philosophy or a religion? Many scholars say that Confucianism is a social and ethical

Confucius was a Chinese philosopher who devised moral guidelines for individuals in society.

philosophy and not a religion at all. Confucianism, they point out, is concerned primarily with human life in this world, not with the supernatural, and furthermore has no formal church, priesthood, or creed.

Others argue with equal conviction that Confucianism is a religion. They contend that although Confucianism focuses above all on this-worldly issues such as how to live virtuously or build a harmonious society, it does contain spiritual elements. Confucius may have been reluctant to discuss supernatural issues with his disciples. Nonetheless, say those scholars who consider Confucianism a religion, he was convinced that his mission as a moral teacher came directly from Heaven (the supreme Chinese deity). Moreover, they argue, like most religions, Confucianism has its own scriptures—the collected sayings of the sage and his leading disciples as well as the classic works of Chinese literature, which Confucius urged his disciples to study. Confucianism even has rituals and temples associated with it, they point out, although they concede that most of the rituals, such as the great state sacrifices of imperial China, have long since faded away, and that the antique Confucian temples that still dot the East Asian countryside today serve primarily as museums and tourist attractions, rather than centers of a living faith.

It might be most accurate to say that Confucianism has been both a philosophy and a religion at various times in its long history, and that today, although most of the rituals once associated with it have disappeared, Confucianism remains a religion in one key sense: At its core, Confucianism, like the world's other great religious systems, strives to comprehend the ultimate purpose and meaning of human existence.

chapter | one

Confucius: His Life and Times: 551 B.C.–479 B.C.

Although Confucius is one of the most influential figures in world history, remarkably little is known about his life. Most of what is known is gleaned from the *Analects*, a record of Confucius's sayings and opinions that his disciples compiled after his death. Yet if positive evidence concerning the events and circumstances of Confucius's life is meager, learning and knowledge were clearly of paramount importance to him from his earliest years. Indeed, acquiring knowledge and passing on the fruits of that learning to others would form the heart of his entire life's work.

"I Devoted Myself to Learning"

By the end of his life, Confucius was one of China's most respected scholars, and in the centuries after his death, he would come to be honored in his homeland and beyond as the greatest sage of all time. Yet given his family circumstances, it is remarkable that Confucius was able to obtain an education at all.

The Mandate of Heaven

The traditional Chinese concept known as the mandate of Heaven was first formulated by the founders of the Zhou dynasty, who used it to justify their overthrow of the Shang. The ancient Chinese believed that Heaven, their supreme god, bestowed kings with the mandate or authority to rule. The Zhou conquerors added a new twist to this old idea, arguing that when rulers became corrupt, Heaven could revoke their mandate to govern. The last Shang king, the Zhou accused, drank heavily, neglected his state and religious duties, and used methods of unimaginable cruelty to torture and kill any who dared to criticize him. Consequently, the mandate of Heaven had to be transferred to a new and worthier ruling family.

The tradition of the mandate of Heaven long outlived the Zhou dynasty, continuing as a major element in Chinese political and religious thought until the end of the last dynasty, the Qing, in the early twentieth century. For more than two thousand years, the mandate of Heaven provided each new dynasty in China with a justification for taking power.

Confucius was born in 551 B.C. in the state of Lu in northeastern China. Although his given name was Kong Qiu, he came to be known by the honorary title "Kong Fuzi" (Master Kong), or Confucius in its Westernized form. Confucius lived during the period in Chinese history known as the Zhou dynasty. Dynasties, or hereditary ruling houses, governed China during most of the country's long history. Dynasties held power for decades, often centuries, at a time, with new ruling families seizing control by military might. Hundreds of years before Confucius's time, the Zhou clan overthrew the Shang dynasty, the first Chinese dynasty for which there is clear archaeological evidence.

According to tradition, Confucius was descended from the royal house of Shang. At some point, however, his aristocratic ancestors lost both their fortune and their power. They became part of the shi class, people who could claim noble forebears but possessed little land or wealth of their own. Although financially better off than the peasants who made up most of China's population, the shi were typically stuck in low-level government and military jobs. High-ranking official posts were reserved for the small and wealthy noble class.

As a member of the shi class, Confucius's father probably spent his life toiling as a minor military or government official. Apparently, he was able to accumulate little in the way of money or other worldly possessions in the course of his career. For when he died when Confucius was still a young child, the boy and his mother were forced to live in poverty. Years later, Confucius was to tell his disciples: "We were humble and poor when I was young: that's why I can do so many practical things."[1] Yet if Confucius spent much of his childhood learning menial skills that would have been considered beneath the dignity of other boys of aristocratic lineage, he also somehow managed to obtain an education worthy of a Chinese gentleman.

Historians can only speculate on how Confucius received his early academic training. It was next to impossible for a poor boy to receive a good education during Confucius's day. The young scions of noble families typically acquired

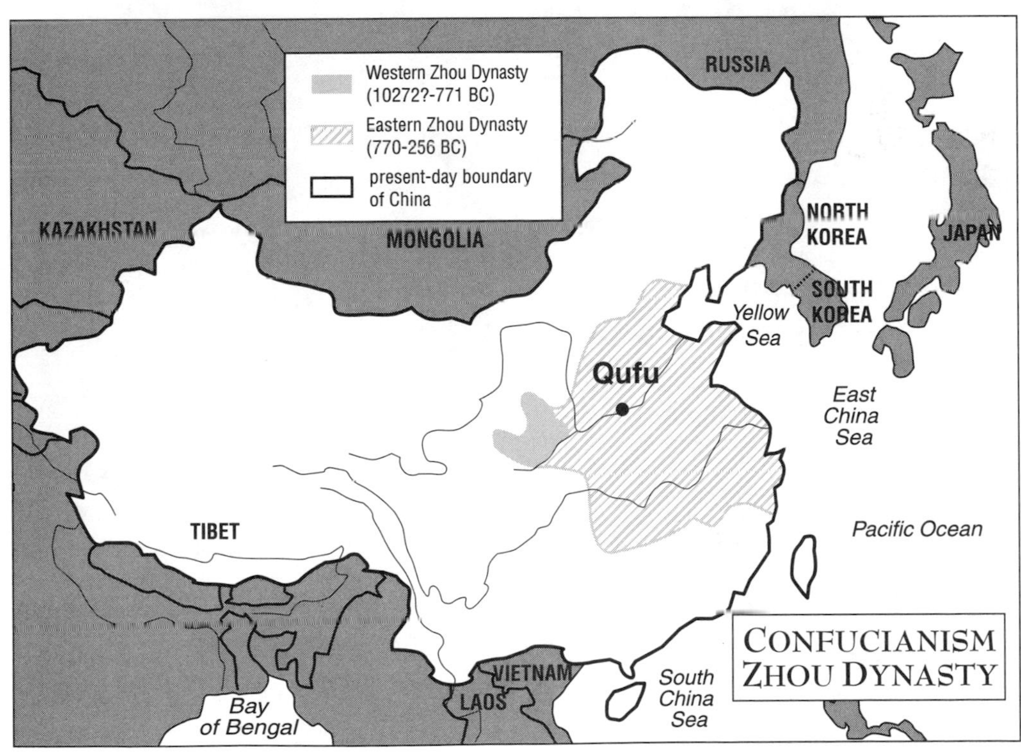

CONFUCIANISM
ZHOU DYNASTY

their education at home. Their wealthy parents could afford to hire private tutors to teach them and, if they were so inclined, their sisters as well. Occa-sionally, the children of less well-off relatives were permitted to join the lessons. This may explain how Confucius was able to secure an education despite his impoverished circumstances. However young Confucius obtained his education, there is every reason to believe that it was a thorough one and that he was a dedicated learner. "At fifteen I devoted myself to learning,"[2] Con-fucius would recall later in life.

Whether he was schooled in the home of an aristocratic relative or self-taught, Confucius's early education probably centered on the Six Arts, the traditional curriculum for noble Chinese boys. A Chinese gentleman was supposed to be well rounded. Consequently, the Six Arts included military skills such as archery and chariot driving in addition to arithmetic, music, and calligraphy, the art of beautiful handwriting. Learning to play a musical instrument was also viewed as an important skill for a man of aristocratic lineage. Confucius, who was particularly fond of music, learned to play a stringed instrument known as the qin, or scholar's lute.

Of all the Six Arts, the most important was li, the traditional Chinese code of rituals and etiquette. In Confucius's day, a deep understanding of and strict adherence to the numerous and complex rules of li was considered the mark of a true gentleman. Li developed centuries before Confucius's birth to guide rulers in performing elaborate sacrifices and other religious ceremonies designed to win the favor of Heaven or to honor ancestors. In time, li evolved into an extremely

A young girl spreads her nimble fingers across the strings of a yue-qin (qin), an instrument similar to one played by Confucius.

detailed set of rules that covered not only formal religious rites but also all the relationships of day-to-day life. Li included rules for how people of different social classes, genders, and ages should address each other, in some instances providing the precise words to use. Even a person's facial expression and gestures were supposed to conform to the model that li set forth.

Worker and Student

Most of Confucius's wealthy male relatives probably continued with their studies of li and the other Six Arts into their twenties, as was customary for young Chinese gentlemen of the era. Confucius, however, was compelled to find full-time employment when he was still in his late teens. At the age of nineteen, Confucius married a young woman who was also descended from an aristocratic family that had fallen upon hard times. Soon the young couple had a son and daughter. To support his growing family, Confucius worked at minor governmental posts in Lu, first as an accountant for the state granary (a building in which surplus grain was stored) and later as an overseer of state pasture lands. As a member of the shi class, he could aspire only to lower-level administrative jobs such as these. Top government positions in Lu, as elsewhere in China, were reserved for the richest, most powerful nobles.

Yet despite the demands of his job and family, Confucius persisted with his studies. Whenever he could find a free moment, he indulged his passion for learning. As evidenced by remarks he made later in life, Confucius spent countless hours poring over the classic Chinese writings of the past. As a government officeholder, Confucius would have had ready access to these and other books. This was no small thing, for few ordinary people owned books in China during the sixth century B.C. Paper and printing would not be invented for centuries to come. Fashioned from long strips of dried bamboo tied together in a bundle with cords, the books of the era were time-consuming to create and unwieldy to handle and store. Consequently, books were comparatively rare during Confucius's lifetime, with libraries generally confined to one of two places: the homes of rich nobles and governmental offices.

From statements he made to his disciples in later years, it is evident that young Confucius was particularly interested in three classic Chinese works. These were the *Book of History (Shujing),* the *Book of*

Confucius searched for knowledge with his study of China's classics.

Changes (Yijing), and the *Book of Poetry (Shijing.)*

The *Book of History* (also called the *Book of Documents*) is a collection of historical writings and government documents, many of which date from the first centuries of the Zhou dynasty. It portrays the early Zhou dynasty as a golden period in Chinese civilization when kings were selfless and just and their people peaceful and content. One ruler whose noble conduct receives particular attention in the *Book of History* is the duke of Zhou, the younger brother of the dynasty's founder. In the *Book of History*, the duke, who acted as regent after his brother's death, is lauded as the embodiment of the ideal ruler—cultured yet modest, firm yet compassionate, and, above all, completely dedicated to the best interests of his subjects. The duke of Zhou and the other early Zhou leaders described in the *Book of History* became Confucius's heroes. To him, they were "sage kings" of unparalleled insight and virtue, representatives of all that was wise and good in Chinese history. "I love the ancients and diligently seek wisdom among them,"[3] Confucius once declared.

The second classic book Confucius studied closely in his youth, the *Book of Changes*, is the traditional Chinese handbook for divination, or foretelling the future. By the time Confucius was born, divination had been a vital part of Chinese culture for more than a thousand years. It was during the early Zhou period that China's ancient divination system was finally written down in the *Book of Changes*, reportedly by command of the king himself. Confucius's deep interest in the book was most likely rooted in its alleged connection to the Zhou sage kings he revered.

The *Book of Poetry* (sometimes translated as the *Book of Odes*) was the third Chinese classic that

Confucius studied carefully. It is a collection of more than three hundred poems from all parts of China, with most dating from early Zhou times. All of the poems were set to tunes, as was customary in ancient China. Ranging from love songs to work chanteys to temple hymns, they tell of the lives of great rulers as well as ordinary people. Confucius, who considered these traditional poems a source of beauty and inspiration, once said that education begins with the *Book of Poetry*.

In common with the *Book of History*, most of the writings in the *Book of Poetry* paint a picture of an idealized past, a time of benevolent leaders and their hardworking yet fundamentally content subjects. One poem describes the life of peasants who toil in the fields of their noble master's estate. In the last stanza, the supposedly carefree peasants celebrate the autumn harvest with a feast held in their lord's house:

> With twin pitchers they hold the village feast,
>
> Killing for it a young lamb.
>
> Up they go into their lord's hall,
>
> Raise the drinking-cup of buffalo-horn:
>
> "Hurray for our lord; may he live for ever and ever!"[4]

The romanticized view of the past found in poems such as this and in the other classic writings Confucius studied was destined to have a profound influence on his thinking. Indeed, Confucius's deep faith in the superiority of the past over his own times would play a crucial role in the next phase of his life when he transformed himself from part-time student to full-time teacher.

Confucius Decides to Teach

When Confucius was in his twenties, an event took place that would change his life forever: His mother died. In accordance with the customs of China's ancient ancestral cult, Confucius devoted the next three years to mourning his deceased parent. At least as far back as the 1300s B.C., a cult of ancestor worship had existed in China. According to the cult, a relative who died was raised to the status of revered ancestor. Ancestors, who lived on in Heaven with the supreme deity, could be counted on to protect family members back on Earth as long as their descendants honored them with special sacrificial rites and lengthy mourning periods. Traditionally, the longest mourning periods—up to three years—were reserved for parents.

Confucius's deep respect for China's cultural legacy made him determined to strictly observe the conventions of the ancestral cult. He gave up his job and all his normal recreational and social activities following his mother's death. During his long period of seclusion, he devoted himself as never before to his studies. Consequently, by the time his three years of mourning were over, Confucius had gained a

Ancestor Worship

Ancestor worship was an integral part of traditional Chinese religion. During Confucius's time, special temples were constructed where ancestors were honored. In later times, many Chinese families erected simple altars to their ancestors in their homes. Sacrificial feasts were offered to ancestors both to venerate them and to bring about their blessings and assistance.

A poem from the ancient *Book of Poetry* describes the celebration that a wealthy family held at their ancestral temple, in which the ancestors are invited to share a feast in return for bestowing good fortune upon their descendants. The following excerpt from the poem is taken from Valerie Hansen's *The Open Empire: A History of China to 1600.*

> The spirits have enjoyed the food and wine
>
> They will cause the lord to have a long life . . .
>
> By son's sons and grandson's grandsons
>
> Shall his line for ever be continued.

A man sits in a meditative pose in a shrine for ancestor worship.

reputation as one of the most learned men in all of Lu. It was Confucius's newfound celebrity as a scholar that permitted him to change the course of his life and embark on a new career, one that would allow him to continue his own passionate pursuit of knowledge and, at the same time, share his vast learning with others. Confucius had decided to teach.

Unquestionably, Confucius's choice of a teaching career was influenced by his own love of learning. "In a village of ten homes, you could certainly find someone who stands by words as faithfully as me, but no one who so loves learning,"[5] Confucius once told his disciples. Yet as profound as his devotion to learning may have been, Confucius had another motive for teaching as well, one rooted in the political and social conditions of sixth century B.C. China.

To Heal an Ailing Society

Confucius lived in a period of tremendous unrest when the old social and political institutions of feudal China were breaking down and new ones had not yet been created to replace them. Feudalism is a political, social, and economic system based on bargains made between sovereigns and their vassals, or noble subjects. China's feudal system was created by the earliest Zhou rulers to help them rule their vast new domain. After splitting their realm into a number of different feudal states, the Zhou monarchs permitted local lords—relatives or trusted allies—to govern them in return for their allegiance and for certain services, the most crucial being military assistance.

At first, the vassals served their Zhou rulers loyally. By the time of Confucius's birth in the sixth century B.C., however, the feudal system that the Zhou founders built was crumbling. Local lords had begun raising armies of their own, compelling thousands of peasants to serve as their foot soldiers. As the lords became increasingly independent and powerful, the Zhou kings were reduced to figureheads. The ineffective monarchs could only watch helplessly as their vassals used their private armies to battle each other for land and influence.

The nearly constant warfare among rival nobles took a devastating toll on the Chinese. Tens of thousands of men, women, and children were slaughtered. Brutal warlords ordered mass beheadings; in some regions, entire villages were wiped out. High taxes designed to pay for the fighting

A Zhou dynasty emperor, accompanied by footmen, rides through the countryside in his horse-drawn chariot.

placed an onerous burden on the peasants, who made up most of China's population. Leaders seemed indifferent to the needs of their people, and corruption was rampant at all levels of government.

Confucius abhorred the savagery and corruption of his times. One of the smallest and weakest of the feudal states, Confucius's home state of Lu was invaded repeatedly by its larger neighbors. To make matters worse, dishonest and opportunistic men dominated Lu's government. Confucius looked back longingly to the golden days of the early Zhou dynasty portrayed in the classic Chinese works he had studied so closely. He wanted to help return his country to that legendary era of honesty, peace, and civility. Yet the question was, how?

It is hardly surprising that a man as devoted to learning as Confucius would conclude that the solution to his society's problems lay in education. Confucius became determined to teach his compatriots the accumulated wisdom of the past as a means of healing his ailing nation. He would train the rising generation in the moral values, rituals, and culture of the Zhou founding fathers as set forth in the ancient Chinese classics. Once they had mastered the wisdom of the forefathers, he would send his students out into their troubled nation to reform it. As government officials and schoolmasters, parents, and community members, they would pass on the knowledge and ethical values they had learned to others. In this way, Confucius hoped, his disciples would be able to restore to Chinese society the stability, order, and virtue of an earlier and better time.

Confucius firmly believed that the ultimate purpose of education was not merely the betterment of the individual learner, but the improvement of society as a whole. Thus, in the very first sentence of the *Analects,* Confucius asks his disciples: "To learn, and then, in its due season, put what you have learned into practice . . . isn't that a great pleasure?"[6] For Confucius, knowledge was not just something to be acquired; it was something to be used for the benefit of all.

Confucius's School and Students

The school that Confucius founded to teach China's youth the wisdom and moral values of the past bore little resemblance to schools today. For one thing, all of Confucius's students were male—most Chinese assumed that girls required only the most basic education to prepare them for their preordained roles as wives and mothers. For another, the atmosphere in Confucius's school was highly informal, with lessons structured around question and answer sessions instead of lectures, tests, or term papers. The emphasis was on teaching students how to think rather than what to think. Confucius expected his students to formulate their own answers instead of looking to him to supply them. "I never instruct those who aren't full of passion, and I never enlighten those who aren't struggling to explain themselves," Confucius declared. "If I show you one corner and you can't show me the other three," he told his pupils, "I'll say nothing more."[7]

Confucius built his curriculum around two major subject areas: first, classical Chinese learning and culture including history, poetry, ritual, and music, and second, practical morality. Confucius stressed a deep knowledge of the *Book of History, Book of Poetry,* and other ancient Chinese writings in the first part of his curriculum. In the second, he relied primarily on teaching by example, striving to make his personal conduct a model for his students to emulate.

Confucius was especially concerned with training his students for government service. He was convinced that learned and virtuous men had the power to transform their communities by their words and actions no matter what their vocations might be. Nonetheless, he placed particular faith in the ability of ministers, advisers, and other high-level government officials to better society. Knowledgeable and morally upright administrators would provide an ideal for ordinary people to emulate. They would also exert a vital civilizing influence on the aristocratic leaders of China's various feudal states, persuading them to throw aside their selfish and violent ways in favor of the old values of the legendary sage kings—namely, honesty, justice, propriety, and compassion.

Confucius hoped that the civil servants he trained would view their work as a sacred calling, rather than merely a means to power and wealth. While high-minded people "cherish Integrity" and "are clear about duty," Confucius taught his students, morally inferior or "little people" cherish "territory" and "are clear about profit."[8] Far too many of China's feudal rulers were land-grabbing tyrants, dedicated only to their own personal gain, Confucius believed. In their roles as advisers and ministers, his students would teach the unscrupulous lords another mode of governing and of living

A Confucian Holy Book written in both English and Chinese guides the individual in compassion, honesty, propriety, and justice.

based on the ethics and wisdom of an earlier, more enlightened era.

Little is known about these young men for whom Confucius harbored such lofty expectations. Legend says that Confucius instructed three thousand pupils during the course of his teaching career. Most of them probably came to Confucius for instruction when they were in their early twenties; a few seem to have made a career of studying with Confucius, remaining with him until he was elderly and they were well into middle age. Many others went on to successful careers in government and teaching after studying with Confucius for several years. Of the twenty-two students mentioned by name in the *Analects*, "at least half . . . ultimately held government posts; some of these were quite important,"[9] writes H. G. Creel. Of the remaining students named in the *Analects*, reports Creel, a large number became teachers, including several who were tutors of important rulers.

Almost certainly, those students of Confucius who attained important government positions came from aristocratic families because throughout the course of Confucius's lifetime, nobles continued to monopolize the highest official posts in China. Confucius's school attracted students from some of the most prominent families in his hometown of Qufu. As his reputation as a scholar and teacher spread, the wealthy scions of aristocratic clans from all corners of Lu and from neighboring states flocked to Qufu to study under the learned Master Kong.

Yet, if many of Confucius's pupils were aristocrats, the Master refused to make high social and economic status prerequisites for admission to his school. Confucius's willingness to accept any student, regardless of wealth or family background, signaled a significant break with tradition. Education in China had always been the exclusive domain of the well off or, at the very least, the well-connected. Although the majority of Confucius's pupils came from families that were at least prosperous enough to spare their labor in the fields, a few of his disciples were almost completely destitute. On occasion, Confucius waived all admission fees for a promising but penniless student, even allowing impoverished pupils to live with him and his family until their education was completed. "I never refuse to teach anyone, not even those so lowly they come offering nothing [as tuition] but a few strips of dried meat,"[10] Confucius once declared. As the product of an impoverished family himself, Confucius was determined to make education available to motivated and talented young men of all backgrounds, no matter how humble.

Although Confucius did not require his students to possess high social or economic standing, he did expect them to be unfailingly honest, polite, and compassionate toward others. Above all, he wanted them to be as totally dedicated to their studies as he had always been to his own. "Study as if you'll never know enough," he admonished his pupils, "as if you're afraid of losing it all."[11] Confucius once described himself as a man so full of passion for learning that he sometimes "forgets to eat."[12] He expected no less of his students.

Confucius, immortalized in this statue, instilled the value of learning in his students, emphasizing how to think rather than what to think.

Among his many pupils, Confucius believed the one most devoted to his studies was a peasant named Yen Hui. No one possessed such a "true love of learning" as Yen Hui, the Master avowed. Moreover, according to Confucius, Yen Hui was a model of virtue: "He never blamed others [for his errors] and never made the same mistake twice."[13] Confucius particularly admired his student's stoicism in the face of terrible poverty. "How noble Yen Hui is!" he said. "To live in a meager lane with nothing but some rice in a split-bamboo bowl and some water in a gourd cup—no one else could bear such misery. But it doesn't even bother Hui. His joy never wavers."[14]

A Government Position

Confucius clearly derived enormous satisfaction from teaching, especially when he was able to instruct students like Yen Hui who shared his own deep passion for learning. Nonetheless, Confucius dreamed of obtaining a high-level government post. As a top-level administrator or adviser to a noble ruler, Confucius thought he could accomplish much to improve his flawed society. He once told his disciples that if a ruler "employed me for even a single year, a great deal could be done. And in three years, the work could be complete."[15]

Confucius finally attained his first important political office when he was in his early fifties, probably through the assistance of one of his aristocratic disciples. Around 500 B.C., Confucius was appointed chief magistrate of the town of Zhongdu. Confucius immediately devoted himself to making the townspeople adhere to the detailed rituals and strict moral codes of early Zhou times. In line with ancient standards regarding the segregation of the sexes, he insisted that women and men walk on opposite sides of the street. He hammered away at the importance of honesty so persistently that if a citizen accidentally dropped his wallet, the wallet was left untouched where it had fallen—sometimes for days—until its owner returned for it.

Confucius soon came to the attention of the duke of Lu who promoted him to a new and even more influential post—minister of justice for Lu, the highest government position that a man from the lesser aristocracy could hold. Confucius's tenure in office was destined to be short, however. His unswerving devotion to ancient rules and ethical codes quickly alienated the duke's other ministers and advisers. According to one account, they plotted to get rid of Confucius by hiring eighty courtesans (prostitutes who associated with aristocratic men) to pose as a gift to the duke from another ruler. When the duke refused to heed Confucius's advice to return this decadent offering, Confucius resigned his position in disgust. He could not have realized it at the time, but his political career had just ended. Confucius "seems to have been temperamentally unfitted to achieve any marked success as a statesman," remarks the scholar D. Howard Smith. "In an age when courts were places of intrigue and men won the favor of princes by flattery . . . Confucius was out of place, for he could be mordant [cutting] in criticism, and his blunt honesty and native uprightness were a reproach to the devious politicians with whom he had to associate."[16]

Final Years

After his disheartening experience with the duke of Lu and his unscrupulous ministers, Confucius decided to abandon his home state. Traditionally called "the time of wandering," Confucius's self-imposed exile was to last for nearly fourteen years. During those years, the Master traveled through the states of central China, accompanied by a small band of faithful students.

In each town Confucius visited, he pleaded with the local rulers to turn their backs on corruption and warfare and uphold the traditional ritual and moral codes of the past. Although he was respected as a great scholar by many of the officials with whom he conversed, none offered him a permanent job or made any serious attempt to put his

The Five Classics

Several centuries after Confucius's death, the *Book of Changes, Book of Poetry, Book of History, Spring and Autumn Annals,* and an additional book titled the *Book of Rites* became the heart of the Confucian canon of scriptures. These five works were known as the Five Classics, or *Wujing.*

Although there is ample evidence that Confucius closely studied the *Book of Changes, Book of Poetry,* and *Book of History,* many historians doubt the traditional claim that he edited these books during the last years of his life. Philosophical commentaries included in the *Book of Changes* once ascribed to Confucius are now believed to have been written long after his death in the third century B.C. The traditional claim that Confucius personally selected the approximately three hundred works included in the *Book of Poetry* from a group of several thousand poems also appears to be unfounded. That editing process, historians now think, probably occurred well before Confucius was born.

Confucius has also been credited with editing the *Book of Rites,* which details gentlemanly etiquette and the rules for weddings, funerals, and other important social and religious events. Modern scholarship, however, indicates that the manual was probably put together during the Han dynasty (202 B.C.–A.D. 220) from earlier writings. Many contemporary historians also dispute the long-held belief that Confucius compiled the *Spring and Autumn Annals,* a history of his home state of Lu.

ideas into practice. Time after time his hopes were dashed. "Am I to be a bitter gourd left dangling on a string [to dry] and never eaten?"[17] Confucius wondered dejectedly.

In 484 B.C., after almost a decade and a half on the road, Confucius was ready to end his wanderings. Well into his sixties by now, he wanted to live out his final years in his own home. Back in Lu, Confucius resumed his teaching career. Still as hungry for knowledge as ever, Confucius also devoted countless hours to studying the classic works of Chinese literature. According to tradition, he used his deep understanding of Chinese culture and history to edit the *Book of Poetry, Book of Changes,* and *Book of History* and compile a history of Lu entitled *Spring and Autumn Annals* during this period.

These final years were productive yet sad ones for Confucius. First, he lost his only son. Then, Yen Hui, the one disciple Confucius believed truly shared his own unquenchable thirst for knowledge, died. For a time, Confucius fell into despair. "Heaven's killing me! It's killing me!"[18] he lamented.

Confucius's last days came during the summer of 479 B.C. According to the *Analects,* as Confucius lay dying, one of his disciples asked if the Master would like him to pray for him. Confucius declined. "My life has been my prayer,"[19] he replied simply.

For three years after Confucius's death, a small group of his closest disciples kept watch over their master's tomb in Qufu, in accordance with the ancient mourning customs for a deceased parent. When the mourning period was over, the students scattered throughout the state of Lu and beyond, resolved to spread Master Kong's teachings to the people of China.

chapter | two

Confucianism Emerges: The Fifth Through the Third Centuries B.C.

During the first centuries after Confucius's death, a new school of thought developed from his teachings that would eventually come to be known as Confucianism. Confucianism is based on the ideas of Confucius as revealed in the *Analects,* and to a lesser extent, on the ideas of two of Confucius's disciples: Mencius, who lived about one hundred years after Confucius in the fourth century B.C., and Xunzi, who lived in the third century B.C.

Confucius never set out to create a new philosophy or religion. Throughout his life, he insisted that he was not an innovator. Confucius's self-proclaimed mission was to restore his troubled society to an earlier and better time by teaching traditional wisdom and values. "Transmitting insight, but never creating insight, standing by my words and devoted to the ancients,"[20] is how the Master describes himself in the *Analects.*

In fact, Confucius was much more than merely a transmitter of past insights or principles. He developed his own ideas regarding key moral, social, political, and religious issues, including what constituted the supreme virtue, how to achieve an orderly society and a good government, and the nature of the relationship between Heaven and humankind. It was to be these original ideas combined with traditional concepts from the Chinese past, such as filial piety (respect for parents) and li (rites and etiquette), that would form the basis of what came to be called Confucianism.

Confucian Moral Philosophy: Ren and Shu

Above all else, Confucianism is concerned with ethics, or the rules of right and wrong behavior. Confucius was convinced that he lived in a morally bankrupt society and that too many of his compatriots were squandering their time on Earth in a selfish pursuit of money, power, and social status. "Wealth and position—that's what people want,"[21] he told his disciples in disgust. In their headlong rush for riches and rank, he accused, the Chinese people had foolishly tossed aside the traditional virtues, such as duty, propriety, and honesty, that had once made their country great. Confucius hoped to recover these lost virtues of the legendary sage kings.

Yet if Confucius was determined to revive the moral principles of China's supposed golden era, he also introduced an entirely new element to his ethical teachings. A virtue that had received little attention in the past was actually the highest virtue of all and the source from which every other virtue sprang, he asserted. Mentioned well over a hundred times in the *Analects,* Confucius's supreme virtue was ren, often translated as human-heartedness.

Before Confucius, ren was thought to apply only to the aristocracy. It was similar to the Western concept of "noblesse oblige"—the obligation of nobles to offer charity to those below them on the social-economic ladder. Confucius dramatically expanded both the meaning and the importance of ren. Ren applied to every member of society, from the king down to the peasant, he contended. And it meant far more than merely being charitable to the less fortunate. In a nutshell, ren meant compassion for all human beings. When a disciple asked Confucius what he must to do to practice ren, Confucius responded simply: "Love people."[22]

The Master Said: Selections from the *Analects*

The Analects, *or* Lunyu, *means "The Selected Sayings." The book is divided into twenty chapters and 497 verses. All following selections are from the translation by David Hinton.*

• "The Master said: Don't grieve when people fail to recognize your ability. Grieve when you fail to recognize theirs." (1:16)

• "The Master said: In government, the secret is Integrity. Use it, and you'll be like the polestar: always dwelling in its proper place, the other stars turning reverently around it." (2:1)

• "The Master said: At fifteen I devoted myself to learning, and at thirty stood firm. At forty I had no doubts, and at fifty understood the Mandate of Heaven. At sixty I listened in effortless accord. And at seventy I followed the mind's passing fancies without overstepping the bounds." (2:4)

• "The Master said: If you can revive the ancient and use it to understand the modern, then you're worthy to be a teacher." (2:11)

• "The Master said: To learn and never think—that's delusion. But to think and never learn—that is perilous indeed!" (2:15)

• "The Master said: Don't worry if you have no position: worry about making yourself worthy of one. Don't worry if you aren't known and admired: devote yourself to a life that deserves admiration." (4:14)

• "The Master said: Poor food and water for dinner, a bent arm for a pillow—that is where joy resides. For me, wealth and renown without honor are nothing but drifting clouds." (7:16)

• "The Master said: Put the people first, and reward their efforts well." (13:1)

Ren is intimately linked with another key Confucian virtue: shu, or reciprocity, meaning a willingness to see things from the other person's perspective and take their needs and feelings into consideration in whatever one says or does. Five hundred years before Jesus preached his golden rule: "As ye would that men should do to you, do ye also to them likewise," Confucius formulated what has been called the Confucian or silver rule: "Never impose on others what you would not choose for yourself."[23] On another occasion, Confucius expressed this principle in more positive terms: "If you want to make a stand, help others make a stand, and if you want to reach your goal, help others reach their goal."[24]

Confucian Social Philosophy: The Orderly Family and the Orderly Society

A traditional Chinese virtue that Confucius associated closely with ren and shu was filial piety, meaning obedience and respect toward parents. It is by honoring and loving one's own family, especially parents, that one first learns to practice ren and shu and the other core virtues, Confucius asserted. As a person progressed from childhood to adulthood, the selfless concern for others one had developed at home would naturally expand outward to your relationships within the greater community. Thus the "root of Humanity [ren]" is "to honor parents and elders,"[25] the *Analects* declare.

Family had always been highly valued in ancient China. Yet Confucius placed more emphasis than ever before on its importance, making stable family life the very heart of his social philosophy. When all family relationships are properly ordered, he asserted, then society would be orderly and harmonious. Disorderly families, on the other hand, invariably led to disorderly societies.

Reflecting the conservative attitudes of the culture in which he lived, Confucius assumed that the well-ordered family was hierarchical and patriarchal: Wives must obey their husbands, children submit to their fathers, and younger brothers defer to older brothers.

Confucius believed a stable family life would translate into an orderly, harmonious society.

Sons were especially critical in the Confucian family hierarchy, for they not only carried on the family name but also were responsible for performing the ritual offerings to honor ancestors. By making the ancestral rites that sons traditionally carried out an integral part of filial piety, Confucius attached more weight than ever before to the son's role within the family. When a student asked him how he as a son could best honor his parents, Confucius replied: "In life, serve them according to Ritual," meaning to follow the customary rules of propriety toward parents, such as serving them drink and food first or remaining standing until they were seated. "In death, bury them according to Ritual," he went on. "And then," he concluded, "make offerings to them according to Ritual."[26]

Closely linked to Confucius's understanding of the well-ordered family and its paramount importance to society was his concept of the "Five Relationships," or five basic loyalties among human beings. In keeping with both his emphasis on filial piety and his traditional patriarchal views, the first and strongest of Confucius's five core relationships is the one between father and son. The other basic relationships are those between sovereign (ruler) and subject, husband and wife, older and younger sibling, and friend and friend. Within each of these five relationships, the younger or lower-ranking individual is expected to defer to the older or higher-ranking one, in accordance with age-old Chinese assumptions regarding the hierarchical nature of human society.

Yet whereas subordinates owe their superiors respect and obedience, Confucius argued that superiors also have obligations to those beneath them in the social pyramid, a revolutionary idea for his time and culture. In an era when the rights of the privileged and powerful few were assumed to hold precedence over the rights of the many, Confucius taught that in a truly just and harmonious society, those who hold sway over others—whether rulers or landlords or fathers—must treat their subordinates with compassion and consideration at all times. Only then would they prove themselves worthy of their privileged position.

To better explain the duty of the superior members to their subordinates within society's five basic relationships, Confucius developed another concept. This concept, which came to be known as the "rectification of names," taught that people can build orderly and harmonious societies only when they clearly understand the duties associated with each of the basic relationships and strive to fulfill these duties to the best of their abilities. According to Confucius's rectification of names theory, the father should strive to "rectify," or live up to his title by providing for his sons' educational or vocational training and teaching them virtue, etiquette, and reverence for tradition and authority. In turn, to be worthy of their names, sons must be the best children they can be to their fathers by obeying them, caring for them and their mothers in old age, and honoring their deceased parents and ancestors with the customary rites. Younger friends could best fulfill their obligations to older friends by showing respect for them through using certain prescribed forms of address, bowing, and serving them food and drink first.

Li: Confucius Gives New Importance to an Ancient Concept

The relationship between younger and older friends, like each of the other four basic Confucian relationships, required expertise in li, the traditional Chinese rules of social decorum and ritual. From the beginning, li was a key component of Confucianism. Since it allegedly originated with the ancient sage kings whom he revered, Confucius naturally valued li highly. Yet he also envisioned an important new role for it, one closely linked to his concerns for his ailing society. Confucius asserted that li had a profoundly civilizing influence on human beings, promoting a sense of dignity and compassion among them. This was no small matter for a man who lived in violent and unsettled times when civility and kindness were in markedly short supply.

Confucius himself was meticulous in observing the customary etiquette and rites of li. When visiting the residence of a noble ruler, he would assume a cringing position in adherence with the ancient rules. "Entering the palace gates, he closed in on himself, as if the gates weren't big enough,"[27] according to the *Analects*. He was equally careful about his behavior at home and in his community. "If the mat wasn't laid straight, he wouldn't sit,"[28] the *Analects* declare. "Whenever he met someone in mourning garments," the book's authors note, "his expression turned solemn. . . . For those in mourning and those carrying official documents, he bowed down to the crossbars of his carriage."[29]

Placing as much value as he did on li, Confucius was deeply disturbed by the tendency of some of his contemporaries to treat ancestral rites and other traditional religious ceremonies as mere formalities. He may have even feared that their casual attitude toward the ancient rites would eventually cause a vital part of the li heritage to fade out of Chinese life altogether. Sacrifice to your ancestors as if you believe they are actually present, Confucius admonished his students. "Ritual without reverence, mourning without grief—how could I bear to see such things?"[30] he once asked.

Confucian Political Philosophy: The Good Ruler and the Good Official

Confucius and his followers were convinced that the proper performance of li was especially vital for rulers. Both the sovereign and the entire country would prosper if he carried out all his official duties, and especially the traditional state religious rites, in accordance with the standards of li that the early Zhou sages set down. Confucians

Confucius showed deep respect for social decorum and rituals such as the traditional wedding procession depicted here.

placed particular emphasis on the ancient concept of the mandate of Heaven. According to the concept, Heaven supposedly bestowed kings with the authority to rule, a mandate that could be removed if the king failed to correctly perform the state religious rituals, and most important, the annual sacrifice to Heaven.

By complying with the rules of li, the king not only fulfilled his sacred obligations to Heaven, Confucianism taught, but also set an important moral example for his subjects to emulate. Rulers profoundly influence their people, for good or ill, Confucius believed. The good king encouraged respect for tradition among his people by strictly following the dictates of li himself. Likewise, he promoted virtue among his subjects by always acting with honesty, justice, generosity, and compassion. If the ruler sets his heart "on what is virtuous and benevolent, then the people will be virtuous and benevolent," Confucius declared. When the sovereign is upright, he said, he "will have the Integrity of wind,"[31] and his subjects will imitate him just as the grass bows before the breeze.

An upright leader, Confucius further argued, will not need to rely on harsh punishments to keep his subjects in line. Indeed, Confucius abhorred the tendency of many rulers of his era to use corporal punishment as a means of control. This method of governing inevitably backfires on a ruler, the Master taught. If you count on "punishment to keep them true, the people will grow evasive and lose all remorse. But if you use Integrity to show them the Way and Ritual to keep them true, they'll cultivate remorse and always see deeply into things,"[32] he declared. In other words, rulers who depend on harsh punishments or intimidation to govern will find that their subjects lack a well-developed conscience or sense of shame. What they possess instead is a talent for not getting caught when they have done wrong. In contrast, if a ruler governs by his moral suasion, his subjects will develop strong consciences and want to do what is right.

Although Confucius's ideas regarding the superiority of moral example over harsh punishments were innovative for his time and culture, his assumption that the supreme ruler would be a hereditary monarch descended from aristocratic ancestors clearly reflected traditional attitudes. Confucius did break with tradition, however, in his conception of the kind of men who

A Chinese civil servant who was educated and showed moral virtue was seen as well-qualified for public office.

should be appointed as the supreme ruler's top officials. Although the highest governmental positions in China were held by members of the nobility during Confucius's era, he insisted that the ruler's ministers and top advisers need not be aristocrats. A well-rounded education combined with unwavering moral virtue, not lofty social rank, was what qualified men for political office, Confucius believed. In effect, he sought to replace China's traditional aristocracy with a moral and intellectual meritocracy, in which men earned political office on the strength of their character and abilities. In another break with accepted political practice, Confucius also taught that the emperor should delegate much of his power and administrative responsibilities to these virtuous scholar-officials, instead of keeping all decision making firmly within his own hands.

Junzi was the word Confucius used to describe the kind of men best suited to advise the ruler and help him in the day-to-day running of the government. In the past, the term *junzi* had referred to a prince or noble. To Confucius, however, junzi meant something very different. According to him, a junzi was a morally and intellectually superior person or "noble-minded one," as the word is sometimes translated. The Confucian junzi possesses both the wisdom to tell right from wrong and the courage to behave accordingly. Even though the Chinese government had traditionally been run for the benefit of the rulers, the Confucian junzi understands that the true purpose of government is to serve the people and is therefore guided in all his actions by a deep concern for the general welfare rather than personal ambition or greed. "Broad-minded" and "not stuck in doctrines"[33] when he discovers that he is wrong, he is not afraid to change. Ever willing to stand up for what he knows is right, if necessary, a junzi will even go so far as to openly challenge his ruler, although it might mean losing his position. "What good are counselors who don't steady [their ruler] when he's stumbling?"[33] Confucius once asked. If a ruler's policies are unjust, and none of his advisers or ministers speak up in opposition, the Master warned, such cowardice could be enough to destroy the entire state.

Confucian Religious Thought: Heaven and Humankind

As the Master's emphasis on creating good government and an orderly, harmonious society reveals, Confucianism is primarily concerned with life in this world. Above all, Confucius sought to understand and improve the human condition by studying the wisdom of the past and, in some cases, by expanding and reinterpreting that cultural and intellectual legacy. Confucianism's this-worldly orientation has led some modern scholars to go so far as to claim that the Master's teachings are totally humanistic and not concerned with spiritual issues at all. Others, however, assert that Confucianism possesses a religious dimension, one that was clearly molded by traditional Chinese beliefs. They point out that Confucius deeply revered the ancestral rites and state ceremonies of ancient Chinese religion. He was invariably meticulous in performing the customary sacrifices and incensed with those who did not show the proper respect or concern for the age-old rites. Moreover, they contend, Heaven, the supreme god of ancient Chinese religion, played a vital part in Confucius's thought.

Indeed, Confucius referred to the ancient deity with great reverence throughout the *Analects*. He makes it clear that he counted on Heaven's protection and understanding and believed that his mission as a teacher and reformer came directly from Heaven itself. At a low moment in his life when he felt forgotten and alone, Confucius comforted himself with the thought that "perhaps Heaven, at least, understands me."[35] On another occasion, he told his disciples that every human being was accountable to the supreme deity, warning: "Once you've offended Heaven, there's nowhere to turn."[36] Confucius's belief that his mission to help heal Chinese society was Heaven-sent seems to have given him the strength to meet dangers and disappointments throughout his life. For instance, when Confucius visited the state of Song during his period of wandering, he somehow managed to anger a high government official there named Huan T'ui. After Huan T'ui threatened to have him assassinated, Confucius calmed his frightened disciples, saying: "My Integrity [sometimes translated as "power"] is born of Heaven. So what can Huan T'ui's assassins do to me?"[37]

Linked closely to Confucius's beliefs regarding Heaven was another traditional Chinese idea: the dao. Before Confucius, the Chinese character dao was generally used to denote a path or a way of action. In Confucius's thought, the ancient concept took on a new meaning, one that was firmly rooted in his particular understanding of Heaven. Heaven, Confucius thought, was more than just the creator of the universe; it was also the supreme moral power. Confucius's stress on Heaven as the chief moral power led him, in turn, to interpret the dao as the moral path that Heaven wants all men and women to follow during their time on earth. Predictably, the Confucian dao of Heaven is based on the virtues stressed by the Master, including ren, shu, wisdom, propriety, and honesty. According to the Master and his followers, living one's life according to the dao of Heaven is the highest human duty and the greatest human goal.

Although Confucius taught the vital importance of following the moral path of Heaven, he generally shied away from discussing the supernatural or life after death with his fol-

Confucius interpreted the ancient Chinese concept of the dao to mean the moral path that Heaven expects all people to follow.

lowers, despite the intense popular interest these subjects seem to have generated in his day. Thus when a disciple wondered about "serving ghosts and spirits," Confucius cut him short, demanding: "You haven't learned to serve the living, so how could you serve ghosts?" When the disciple then inquired about death, the Master once again countered with a question of his own: "You don't understand life . . . so how could you understand death?"[38]

Some scholars have taken this reluctance to talk about otherworldly subjects as indifference toward spiritual issues. D. Howard Smith believes, however, that Confucius avoided discussing the supernatural simply because "he saw no point in interminable discussion on questions for which there could be no certain answer."[39] "Shall I explain understanding for you?" Confucius once asked a disciple. "When you understand something, know that you understand it. When you don't understand something, know that you don't understand it. That's understanding."[40]

Mencius: Transmitter and Transformer of Confucius's Teachings

During the decades following his death, Confucius's religious, social, and political teachings were spread and, in some cases, expanded on by his followers. The most important of Confucius's early disciples and interpreters was Mencius (the Westernized form of the name Mengzi), who lived about a century after the Master. Called China's "Second Sage," Mencius is generally recognized as the most influential molder of Confucianism after Confucius himself. Just as Confucius not only transmitted but also transformed the teachings of the ancients in critical ways, Mencius was a transformer as well as a transmitter of the Master's teachings.

Under the influence of his tutor, a former student of Confucius's grandson, Mencius became convinced that he had a mission to spread and defend Confucius's teachings. The task to which he had committed himself was a challenging one, for while Confucianism had had to contend with competing belief systems in China ever since its inception, during Mencius's time, a remarkable array of new philosophies was springing up in the country.

During the fourth century B.C., warfare between rival feudal lords had become even more ferocious than in Confucius's day, with a handful of the most powerful states locked in an all-out contest for supremacy. In these bloody and turbulent times, people were more concerned than ever to uncover a formula for creating a stable society and effective government. A number of different scholars offered their own solutions to China's social and political problems—so many, in fact, that the period came to be known as the era of the "Hundred Schools of Thought." Consequently, Mencius and other Confucians of his era were compelled to vie for the attention and support of rulers and ordinary people alike with scores of other thinkers and teachers, including some who openly ridiculed their ideas.

While Mencius was spreading his young philosophy and defending it against its critics, he was also helping to shape Confucian doctrine in significant ways. Most important, Mencius formulated a clear theory of human nature, something that the Master himself had failed to do. Are human beings born good or evil? Is every person capable of behaving virtuously, and if so, why? Confucius never attempted to answer these

Mencius Defends Confucianism Against Mozi

Mencius was especially concerned with showing Confucianism's superiority over one of the most popular philosophies of his time: Mohism, named for its founder, Mozi. Mozi, who formulated his philosophy in direct response to the Master's teachings, was particularly scornful of Confucius's emphasis on filial piety. Confucians focused too much on the individual's duties toward his family, he said, and not enough on his obligations toward all human beings. In response, Mencius attacked Mozi's principle of universal love as unrealistic. You cannot expect people to feel equal love for everyone, Mencius argued, for a person's affection for another naturally depends on the closeness of the relationship between them. Confucius knew what he was doing when he stressed the reverence of children to parents, Mencius further contended, for if you cannot even cherish your own parents, how can you possibly feel any compassion for strangers? Filial piety, Mencius once said, was the very root of human-heartedness (ren).

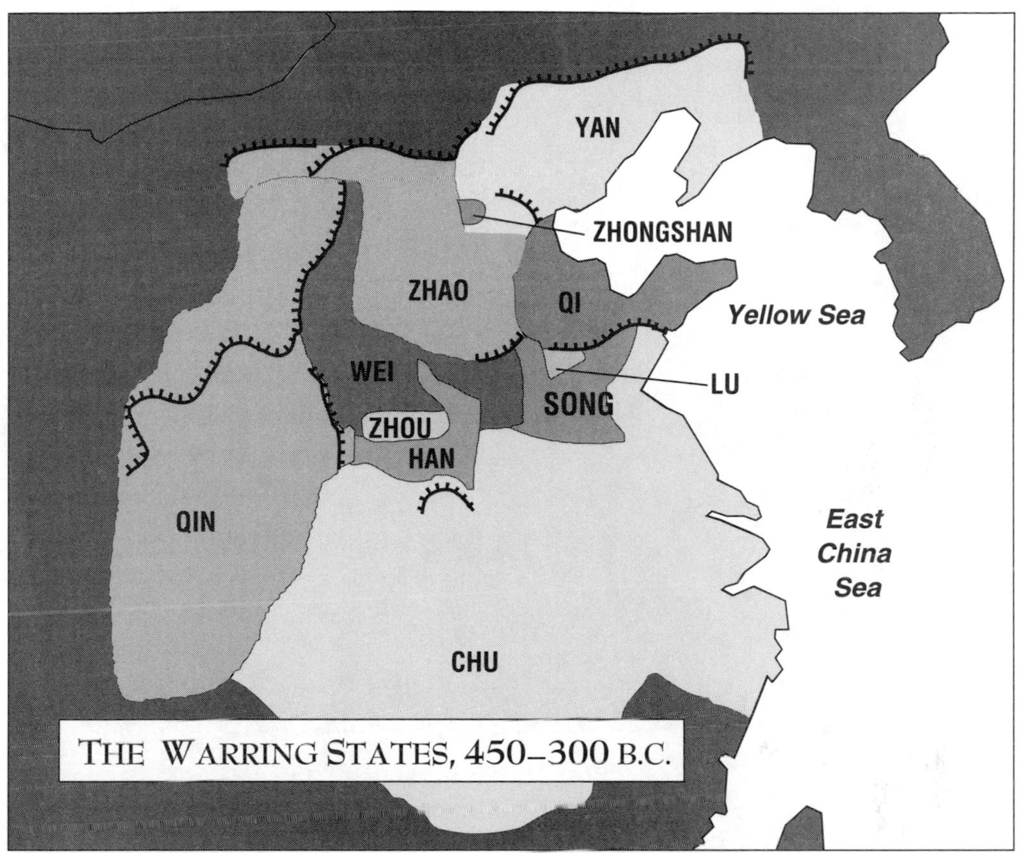

fundamental questions regarding the moral quality of human nature. A century after Confucius's death, Mencius filled that important gap in the Master's teachings by developing a theory of human nature that would eventually become Confucian orthodoxy.

Mencius was deeply optimistic about the human race. All people are naturally virtuous, he asserted. "If left to follow its innate [inborn] feelings," he said, "human nature will do good." In support of his positive view of human nature, Mencius used the example of a small child falling into a well. Anyone observing the drowning child would feel distressed and want to rescue it, for people cannot bear to see the innocent suffer. Therefore, Mencius concluded, all people must contain the seeds of human-heartedness, or ren, within themselves: "The feeling of compassion is common to all men," he argued, and so, too, is "that of right and wrong."[41]

How can there be evil in the world if humans are born good? Mencius answered this question by asserting that bad people either fail to develop their inborn potential for virtue or lose their original nature altogether as a result of a corrupt environment. The way to cultivate one's inborn virtue or get it back once it has been lost, Mencius said, is through moral education and training. Indeed, it was the solemn duty of all people to nurture the goodness within them through studying and then putting into practice the central Confucian virtues such as ren, shu, propriety, and honesty.

Mencius Said: Excerpts from the *Book of Mencius*

After his death, Mencius's teachings were written down in the Book of Mencius, *a record of his conversations with his disciples as well as with various rulers and government officials. Like Confucius, Mencius spent many years traveling around China trying to find a ruler willing to follow his advice. Mencius insisted even more strongly than Confucius that rulers must put the best interests of their subjects first. Rulers who neglected their responsibilities to their people or oppressed and mistreated them, he boldly declared, did not deserve to remain in power. Taking Confucius's teachings regarding the ruler's duty to govern with benevolence and justice to its logical conclusion, Mencius contended that people have the right—even the obligation—to rebel against an immoral leader. The following selections from the* Book of Mencius *are taken from* Sources of Chinese Tradition, *edited by Wm. Theodore de Bary.*

• "Here is the way to win the empire: win the people and you win the empire. Here is the way to win the people: win their hearts and you win the people. Here is the way to win their hearts: give them and share with them what they like, and do not do to them what they do not like. The people turn to a humane ruler as water flows downward or beasts take to wilderness." (4 A:9)

• "Mencius said: There are three things that a feudal lord should treasure—land, people, and the administration of the government. If he should treasure pearls and jade instead, calamity is sure to befall him." (7 B:28)

Mencius expanded the teachings of Confucius by asserting that people possessed innate virtue.

Xunzi: Another Important Shaper of Confucianism

After Mencius, the next most influential interpreter of early Confucianism was Xunzi, who was born around the time of Mencius's death in approximately 300 B.C. Trained as a Confucian scholar, Xunzi became Confucianism's most ardent defender during the third century B.C. when the Zhou dynasty was in its death throes. Yet like Mencius, Xunzi was much more than merely a champion or a transmitter of Confucius's teachings. He also sought to shape the Master's ideas in original ways.

In common with Confucius and Mencius, Xunzi emphasized the cultivation of virtues such as ren, li, and justice for rulers and ordinary people alike. However, he differed from both men on one vital point: Xunzi believed that human nature was fundamentally evil. Because of his belief that human beings naturally tend toward wickedness, Xunzi stressed the need for strict laws and a powerful ruler to help keep people in line. In defense of his views on the importance of strong government and laws, he wrote:

> Men's nature is evil, and the fact is that because of this sage-kings in the past . . . enhanced the severity of punishments in order to restrain men. Remove the authority of the sovereign and the transforming effects of ritual and justice, and watch how men will treat each other. The strong would rob and maltreat the weak, the many would oppress and shout down the few. In no time there would be universal anarchy, everybody destroying everybody else.[42]

Although Mencius's optimistic theory of human nature would eventually overshadow Xunzi's teachings as Confucianism continued to evolve during the centuries after the philosophers' deaths, Xunzi's hardheaded realism had a significant impact on the philosophy. For many years, two schools of thought existed within Confucianism, with the "idealistic Confucians" following Mencius in asserting that human nature was basically good, and the "realistic Confucians" following Xunzi in assuming that people are naturally bad and needed strong laws to keep them in check.

Yet despite their differences, both Mencius's and Xunzi's Confucian followers agreed on one essential point: the supreme importance of education for bettering human society. Strict laws could help to prevent bad behavior, Xunzi taught, but only education could actually reform people by making them understand the importance of doing good for its own sake, and not merely to avoid punishment. Above all, both schools within Confucianism urged that government officials be thoroughly educated in the traditional wisdom, ethics, and culture the Master had cherished. For in line with the founder of their philosophy, all Confucians believed that without the guidance and example of learned and virtuous rulers, ministers, and other officials, a better society would never be realized.

Like Confucius himself, Mencius and Xunzi proved unable to gain the support of the rulers and top officials whom they sought to teach and reform. It would not be until the second century B.C., nearly four hundred years after the Master first formulated his ideas regarding the good government and good society, that his followers would finally be able to achieve any real influence over the political life of their country. But before that time, they would have to endure one of the most trying periods in their philosophy's long history.

chapter | three

The Changing Fortunes of Confucianism in China: The Qin Through the Tang Dynasties: 221 B.C.–A.D. 960

By the time of Xunzi's death in about 230 B.C., China was divided among a small group of warring feudal princes who paid little heed to the king of the expiring Zhou dynasty. Within a decade, the strongest of the various feudal states, the Qin, had managed to overcome its rivals and conquer all of China. Under the Qin, the Chinese people were united into a single centralized state for the first time. But just as the peace Confucius had longed for was finally being achieved in China, the fortunes of the philosophy that had evolved from his teachings were taking a decided turn for the worse.

From the time of Confucius's death in the sixth century B.C. until the ascension of the Qin, Confucianism had remained one of a score of different philosophies vying for the loyalty of the Chinese people. Historians can only speculate regarding the number of its followers during this period, but most believe that Confucianism was one of the best known and respected of the various schools of thought in China. Owing no doubt in large measure to the writings of Mencius and Xunzi, Confucius's reputation as a teacher of extraordinary insight grew steadily among the Chinese throughout the period. Under the new Qin regime, however, Confucianism suffered a serious setback when it became the object of official persecution. Over the next ten centuries, Confucianism would undergo a series of ups and downs, from reaching a nadir under the repressive Qin to being elevated to the state ideology under their Han successors, to being partially eclipsed by two popular movements—Buddhism and religious Daoism—during the turbulent Period of Disunity that followed the Han dynasty, and finally, to achieving a comeback under the last ruling house of the period, the Tang.

A Low Point for Confucianism: The Qin Era

Confucianism found itself fighting for its very survival under the ruthless Qin dynasty, which united the country in the late third century B.C. At the root of Confucianism's troubles under the Qin rulers was the Qins' overarching desire to consolidate their control over their huge new realm. Determined to break the might of China's noble warlords, the first Qin emperor, Shi Huangdi, threw out the old Zhou feudal system and split the country into provinces administered by governors who served strictly at his pleasure. That accomplished, he launched the next phase of his campaign to strengthen his hold over the new Chinese empire: the persecution of any individuals or groups who dared to challenge his despotic practices or the authoritarian philosophy known as Legalism, which he had adopted as the imperial ideology. It was inevitable that Confucians would become one of the emperor's main targets. Their insistence that government existed above all to serve the people stood in direct opposition to the teachings of Legalism, which made the interests of the state paramount.

In 213 B.C. Shi Huangdi ordered what would become one of the most infamous acts in Chinese history: the burning of all books in the empire that did not conform to Legalist doctrines. Confucian writings were featured prominently in the decree, and those Confucian scholars who attempted to save their books from destruction were publicly tortured and executed. Yet the Qins' violent crusade to silence their opponents was destined to backfire. Their persecution of the Confucians and other groups whose ideas they disliked outraged the Chinese people, who soon rose up in rebellion. Within a few decades

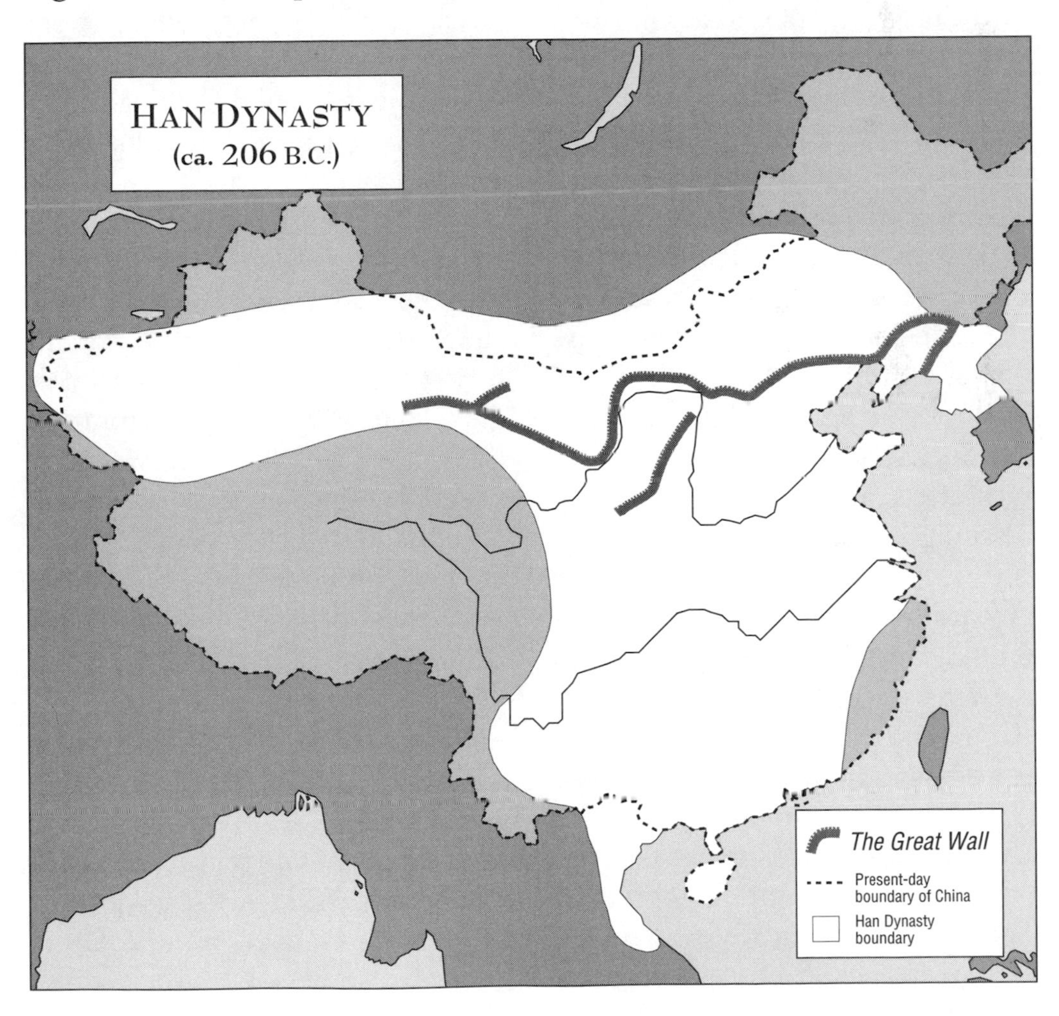

of its creation, the Qin dynasty had fallen and imperial China had a new ruling house, the long-lived Han dynasty (206 B.C.–A.D. 220). A new era was about to begin for Confucianism.

Confucianism Under the Han: The New State Doctrine

Although the new Han rulers relied on a strong, centralized administrative system to govern their realm based on the one created by the Qin, they totally abandoned their predecessors' unpopular reign of terror against ideas, permitting the Confucians and China's numerous other philosophical groups to reestablish themselves. Since countless Confucian writings had been damaged or lost during the Qin era, the Confucian scholars saw their first task after the Han took power, as rescuing and restoring as many of the surviving texts as possible. According to legend, they discovered a complete manuscript of the *Analects* concealed in the walls of the Kong family home in Qufu, where it had been hidden from Qin officials. Despite the efforts of the Confucian scholars, however, some writings could not be located. Fortunately, Confucian scholars were in the habit of learning their classic texts by heart, and thus were able to reproduce from memory large portions of those books that had apparently disappeared for good. In one remarkable case, a ninety-year-old Confucian scholar named Feng Sheng dictated to his daughter the entire text of the *Book of History* from memory.

While some Confucian scholars struggled to restore their philosophy's literary legacy, others were gaining influence within the Han government as high-level advisers and administrators. The willingness of the Han to appoint Confucians to top government posts was probably based on a number of factors, including the Confucians' deeply held belief that public officials should serve their leaders (if virtuous) with the utmost loyalty and devotion. Some historians, however, have suggested that the one thing that probably most attracted the Han emperors to the Confucians was their close association with li—the traditional Chinese code of ritual and etiquette that Confucius emphasized in his teachings. According to the scholar Christian Jochim, the Han rulers were drawn to the pomp and splendor of the elaborate court ceremonies of China's past. This, in turn, proved a tremendous boon for the Confucians, since they were their country's recognized experts in these complex ceremonies as well as in all aspects of li. "While they also held much else in their hand," writes Jochim of the Confucians, their profound knowledge of li was "their trump card. In fact, where early Han emperors were concerned, the Confucians' advice on ritual matters was at least as important as their advice on political ones."[43]

By the reign of the sixth Han ruler, Wu Di, Confucian advisers and administrators had achieved such deep influence within the imperial government that they managed to persuade the emperor to make Confucianism China's official ideology. In 136 B.C. Emperor Wu formally announced that Confucianism alone of all China's numerous schools of thought would receive state sponsorship. Soon after, he directed that a national university be built in the Han capital, at which the most talented students from all over the empire were to be trained in the core Confucian texts. In particular, they were to focus on five classic Chinese books

Confucianism Becomes the State Doctrine

Wu Di's decision to make Confucianism the official doctrine of the Chinese empire was probably linked to the influence of his close adviser, the Confucian scholar and philosopher Dong Zhongshu. Before Wu Di formally announced Confucianism's new position as the official orthodoxy, he received a written recommendation from Dong Zhongshu advising him to appoint only Confucians to government posts and make Confucianism the basis of the state educational system. In his proposal, which is reprinted in Wm. Theodore de Bary's *Sources of Chinese Tradition,* Dong Zhongshu supported his case for Confucianism by arguing that if the Chinese empire was ever to achieve lasting order and stability, its thought had to be unified. The "teachers of today have different doctrines and . . . their principles do not agree. Thus the ruler has no means by which to achieve unity, the laws and institutions undergo frequent changes and the people do not know what to honor," Dong Zhongshu told the emperor. In order that "unity be achieved, the laws be made clear, and the people know what to follow," he therefore asserted that all philosophies other than Confucianism "should be suppressed and not allowed to continue further."

that had become closely associated with the Master and his disciples over the past four centuries: the *Book of History, Book of Poetry, Book of Changes, Book of Rites,* and *Spring and Autumn Annals.* Over time, these five books would come to be known throughout China simply as the "Five Classics."

During the course of the Han era, the national university that Wu founded with its Confucianism-based curriculum, grew steadily until by the end of the dynasty in the early third century A.D., the school enrolled approximately thirty thousand students. To complement the work of the national university, a network of state-funded schools was established throughout the empire, each with a curriculum firmly grounded in the Confucian canon. And at the same time that Confucianism was coming to dominate China's educational system, it was also becoming ever more deeply entrenched in the empire's expanding bureaucracy, a phenomenon that would have greatly pleased the Master.

Since Confucius had stressed the vital importance of reforming and improving society through means of government service, most of the Confucian scholars who attended the national university and other state schools naturally sought a career in government upon graduation. Under Emperor Wu, a competitive examination system was developed to determine their suitability—and that of all other prospective government officials—for public office. This proved to be a great boon for Confucianism, since the new state examinations were based almost exclusively on the Five Classics of Confucianism, no doubt owing to the influence of Wu's Confucian advisers. The Confucianism-based testing system created under the Han did much to cement the philosophy's position in the empire, assert Ch'u and Winberg Chai, for through this system, "the Confucian scholars secured a firm grip on the country's bureaucracy and at the same time also firmly established their hold on China's intellectual life."[44]

Han Confucianism: The Continuing Evolution of Confucian Thought

More than just the political fortunes of Confucianism were changing as the philosophy was in the process of attaining its privileged place within the bureaucracy and state-sponsored educational system of Han China. Its teachings were also being transformed in significant ways. In large part because of the influence of the Confucian scholar-official Dong Zhongshu, Confucianism became tinged with ideas from other Chinese schools of thought during the Han era, particularly the yin/yang and Five Elements philosophies. By borrowing concepts from these popular belief systems, Dong Zhongshu and other Han philosophers were able to broaden Confucianism's appeal for their contemporaries, thereby helping to ensure that the philosophy would endure in changing times.

This traditional Chinese symbol represents the concept of yin/yang, the harmony and balance in nature.

On the eve of the Han era in China, notes D. Howard Smith, "interest was growing in questions relating to the nature of the universe"[45]—questions the Master had largely disregarded but which other Chinese philosophies such as the yin/yang and Five Elements schools had attempted to answer. Desiring to strengthen their philosophy at the expense of its rivals, the Han Confucians grafted yin/yang and Five Elements ideas regarding the workings of nature onto their own tradition.

According to yin/yang theory, all natural occurrences result from the interaction of two opposite yet complementary forces—yin, which is female, dark, and passive, and yang, which is masculine, bright, and active. For the world and all its inhabitants to function harmoniously, yin and yang must remain in constant balance. Related to the yin/yang concept is another traditional Chinese belief—that all things in the universe are made up of five elements—wood, fire, earth, metal, and water, each of which, in turn, is linked with a number of correspondences—for example, a certain color, location, planet, or grain. Like yin and yang, the five elements and their correspondences must continually balance each other if harmony is to be maintained within nature. Dong Zhongshu and his fellow Han Confucians found a way to incorporate these widely accepted ideas into their tradition by arguing that harmonious and successful societies are founded both on their members' commitment to core Confucian virtues like ren and filial piety and on their ability to understand and live in accordance with the natural patterns set forth by the yin/yang and Five Elements schools.

Confucianism in the Period of Disunity: The Rise of Religious Daoism and Buddhism

During the Han era, Confucians were able to effectively meet the challenges posed to their philosophy by competing schools of thought, first and foremost by their ability to achieve a central role in the state bureaucracy and educational system, but also by their resourcefulness in expanding their tradition to include rival ideas such as yin/yang and Five Elements concepts. During the three and a half centuries of disunity and bloodshed that followed the downfall of the Han ruling house, however, Confucians found the challenges presented by two enormously popular new rivals—religious Daoism and Buddhism—more difficult to overcome. For during this turbulent period in Chinese history, Daoism and Buddhism were able to meet the emotional and spiritual needs of the Chinese people in ways that Confucianism could not.

The Period of Disunity began when the Chinese empire splintered into a number of rival states following the overthrow of the Han in A.D. 220. Political instability, almost constant warfare, and widespread famines brought deep uncertainty and misery to the lives of countless Chinese. In these difficult times, many turned away from Confucianism, seeking comfort in the teachings of two relatively new systems of belief in China, religious Daoism and Buddhism.

Daoism had begun not as a religion but as a philosophy in the sixth century B.C. Based on the teachings of the legendary Chinese sage Laozi, philosophical Daoism focuses on the ancient concept of the dao, or way, which Laozi interpreted as the source and unity of life. By the Period of Disunity, Daoism was in the midst of a major transformation, evolving from a philosophy whose appeal was mainly limited to a scholarly elite, to a popular religion, capable of attracting followers from all educational and social backgrounds. While Confucianism still concerned itself above all with life in this world, particularly with

Ban Zhao and Her *Lessons for Women*

One of the most famous Confucian scholars of the Han era was a woman named Ban Zhao. Born into a wealthy Confucian clan, Ban Zhao devoted herself to studying her family's vast book collection. When her brother died before he could finish an official history of the Han, Ban Zhao completed the work for him. The emperor was so impressed by Ban Zhao's scholarship that he asked her to supervise the education of his young empress. While serving in this position, Ban Zhao wrote *Lessons for Women,* the book for which she would become best known. This advice manual for young, unmarried women was read by countless Chinese girls right up until the early twentieth century.

Lessons for Women reflected Ban Zhao's deeply held Confucian beliefs. Like the strongly patriarchal society in which it developed, Confucianism taught that women should be subservient to men. In line with the traditional Confucian view, Ban Zhao advised her readers to practice the three "obediences": to their father before marriage, their husband after marriage, and their oldest son in widowhood; and the four main virtues, which were in essencc: knowing your place, not talking too much, keeping up your appearance for your husband, and mastering such domestic duties as weaving and cooking. However, Ban Zhao broke with Confucian teachings on one key point: Her ideal woman was well educated. In *Lessons for Women,* Ban Zhao made a strong plea for equal education, even though female education was a cause the Master himself never espoused. The following excerpt is from Valerie Hansen's *The Open Empire*.

> [O]nly to teach men and not to teach women—is that not ignoring the essential relation between them? According to the *[Book of] Rites,* it is the rule to begin to teach children to read at the age of eight years, and by the age of fifteen years they ought then be ready for cultural training. Only why should it not be that girls' education as well as boys' be according to this principle?

Daoism, founded by the Chinese sage Laozi, offered spiritual guidance and the hope of peace in the afterlife.

creating a good government and society, Daoism was becoming increasingly preoccupied with the invisible domain of gods and spirits. In this new form of Daoism, the Chinese masses discovered a source of spiritual and emotional solace that Confucianism, which was almost completely silent on religious matters, failed to offer. The humanistic social, political, and ethical teachings of Confucianism, contends D. Howard Smith, "had very little religious appeal to individuals striving to find a way of rising above the sea of sorrow, suffering and sin in which so many felt themselves to be engulfed."[46] Unlike Confucianism with its this-worldly focus, religious Daoism encouraged people to look beyond the hardships and disappointments of their day-to-day existence to an otherworldly realm where they might find contentment, peace, and even eternal life.

Buddhism, like religious Daoism, also offered China's downtrodden masses the promise of a better existence beyond the grave than the one they had known on Earth. The Master had refused to even discuss the possibility of life after death. Buddhism, in contrast, taught that those who followed the Buddha's teachings would someday be released from the miseries of human existence and attain Nirvana, an eternal state of pure enlightenment and bliss. First imported to China from India during the late Han era, Buddhism and its message of freedom from suffering and death spread rapidly through China during the Period of Disunity. Thousands converted, embracing Buddhist practices such as meditation, and donating whatever they could spare for the construction of the Buddhist temples and monasteries that sprang up all over the Chinese countryside.

Significantly for the political fortunes of Confucianism during the Period of Disunity, Buddhism and religious Daoism did not appeal only to China's oppressed masses. Their spiritual teachings won the hearts and minds of Chinese men and women from all levels of society, including many distinguished scholars and artists. Perhaps influenced by the high regard in which the two religions were held by China's intellectuals, a number of the country's political leaders also embraced Daoism and Buddhism. In the courts of the various warlords who ruled China during the Period

Selections from the *Dao De Jing*

The central text of Daoism is the Dao De Jing, *the collected writings of the legendary founder of the philosophy/religion, Laozi. According to Daoist belief, the dao is the eternal and unchanging principle that unites the universe and all living things and can be understood only through a sort of mystic intuition. The following selection from the* Dao De Jing *is taken from* Sources of Chinese Tradition, *edited by Wm. Theodore de Bary:*

The Dao is empty [like a bowl]
It is used, though perhaps never full.
It is fathomless, possibly the progenitor of all things.
It blunts all sharpness,
It unties all tangles;
It is in harmony with all light,
It is one with all dust.
Deep and clear it seems forever to remain.
I do not know whose son it is,
A phenomenon that apparently preceded the Lord.

of Disunity, the once dominant Confucian scholars were now being forced to compete with Buddhist and Daoist scholars for the attention and patronage of their rulers.

Confucianism's political and intellectual influence during the Period of Disunity was further undercut by the demise of China's civil service examination system. With the downfall of the central government, the Confucianism-based tests that the Han developed to determine the qualifications of prospective bureaucrats fell into disuse. Now that a Confucian education could no longer guarantee a prestigious government post, young Chinese men had far less incentive to study the Confucian canon. Confucianism was losing its once firm grip over Chinese politics and education.

This statue of Buddha is one of many built after Buddhism was introduced from India.

Confucianism Begins to Stage a Comeback: The Tang Era

Despite the strong competition it faced from Daoism and Buddhism during the Period of Disunity, however, Confucian learning was not altogether neglected during the era, for some Chinese scholars continued to discover much of value in the Confucian legacy. Nor were Confucian teachings entirely forgotten within the homes of ordinary Chinese men and women. Although many of them might now worship regularly at a Buddhist or Daoist temple, most still clung to traditional Confucian ideas regarding li (social etiquette and rituals) and the importance of honoring parents and ancestors. Consequently, by the time of China's reunification under the Sui and Tang dynasties in the late sixth and early seventh centuries, Confucianism was still generally thought of as one of China's three main religious-philosophic teachings, along with Daoism and Buddhism.

Perhaps motivated by a desire to build goodwill within their large and

Buddhism and the Wheel of Life

Founded by Gautama Buddha in India in the 500s B.C., Buddhism's first principle, or "Noble Truth," is that life is suffering. At the root of all life's suffering, the Buddha taught, lay the worldly ambitions and cravings of human beings. So long as a person remained focused on earthly pleasures and rewards, he or she will be doomed to be reborn again and again into an existence dominated by pain and sorrow. The only way for an individual to escape this "Wheel of Life" with its endlessly repeating cycles of birth, aging, sickness, and death was to renounce all worldly desires and follow the Eightfold Path of right faith, judgment, conduct, language, livelihood, obedience, memory, and meditation. Then the believer could attain Nirvana, a state of complete bliss and understanding in which the individual soul is absorbed into the great cosmic self, or Universal Soul.

diverse empire, the rulers of the newly reunified Chinese empire adopted a policy of supporting all three of their country's main teachings. During the first decades of the Tang dynasty which was to rule China from 618 to 907, Emperor Taizong established the pattern of toleration for all three belief systems that would remain in place for most of the long Tang era. Taizong donated state funds to build and maintain Buddhist and Daoist temples and monasteries. At the same time, he encouraged Confucian learning by enlarging the national university and opening a host of new provincial schools, all with curricula based largely on the Confucian classics. Taizong and his Tang successors also strengthened Confucianism's role in the central government by surrounding themselves with Confucian advisers and by reviving the civil service examination system. Although the restored examinations were not based exclusively on the Confucian canon, many of their questions centered on the Five Classics and other core Confucian texts.

Based on their preference for Confucian advisers and their revival of the civil service examinations, it appears that the Tang rulers viewed Confucianism as the belief system best suited to meeting the political challenges that a reunited Chinese empire presented. Indeed, of China's three main teachings, Confucianism alone provided a clear and practical political philosophy. Unlike Confucianism, Daoism and Buddhism both encouraged their followers to look inward toward their own spiritual development, rather than focusing their attention outward, on the betterment of human government and society. Buddhism, which strove to transcend politics, failed to offer any sort of coherent political program at all. Daoism did have political teachings, but they were centered on the Daoist concept of wu-wei, literally meaning "inaction." In opposition to the Confucian ideal of a carefully ordered and activist central government, the Daoists taught that the best governments were those that governed the least. "One can hardly imagine a world governed—or *un*governed—according to the completely laissez-faire [hands-off] program of the Taoist [Daoist] philosophers,"[47] notes the modern scholar H. G. Creel. Given their partiality for Confucian-trained advisers and administrators, it seems likely that the Tang emperors would have agreed.

The Tang Rulers and the Cult of Confucius

The Tang rulers' resurrection of the civil service exam system and respect for Confucian learning and political insight did much to enhance Confucianism's position within the reunited Chinese empire. So, too, did their efforts to promote Confucian religious practices through what came to be known as the "cult of Confucius."

The cult of Confucius had its roots in the late Han dynasty when official sacrifices were offered to the Master as a sign of respect to the man whose teachings had come to dominate China's educational system. From the time of Confucius's death, his descendants had offered regular sacrifices in his honor at the family estate in Qufu, in accordance with the traditional practices of China's ancestral cult. In A.D. 59, however, the Han emperor took the veneration of Confucius beyond the confines of the Kong family by decreeing that sacrifices be offered to Confucius at the national university and other state schools throughout the empire.

Largely neglected during the Period of Disunity, the cult of Confucius was revived and strengthened by the Tang rulers, undoubtedly owing to the influence of their numerous Confucian advisers. The Confucian scholar-officials may have seen in the cult a means of bringing greater authority and prestige to their school of thought, thereby allowing it to better compete with its Buddhist and Daoist rivals. In A.D. 630, Emperor Taizong decreed that a Confucian temple be constructed in every province and county in China. Modeled largely on Buddhist temples, the new temples featured statues depicting the Master and his most important disciples, as well as tablets listing their names and those of famous Confucian scholars of the more recent past. Local Confucian magistrates were ordered to offer sacrifices to Confucius in the temples each spring and autumn.

A prayer used as part of the sacrificial rites honoring Confucius reveals the profound admiration in which the Master was held by the Confucian scholar-officials who orchestrated and performed the ceremonies:

> O Great teacher, thy virtue surpasses that of a thousand sages,
> And thy way excels that of a hundred kings. . . .
> The reverent and constant observance of thy moral teaching is the expression of our gratitude to thee. Mayest thou enjoy this sacrifice.[48]

Despite the deep reverence displayed for the Master in its prayers and rituals, however, most modern

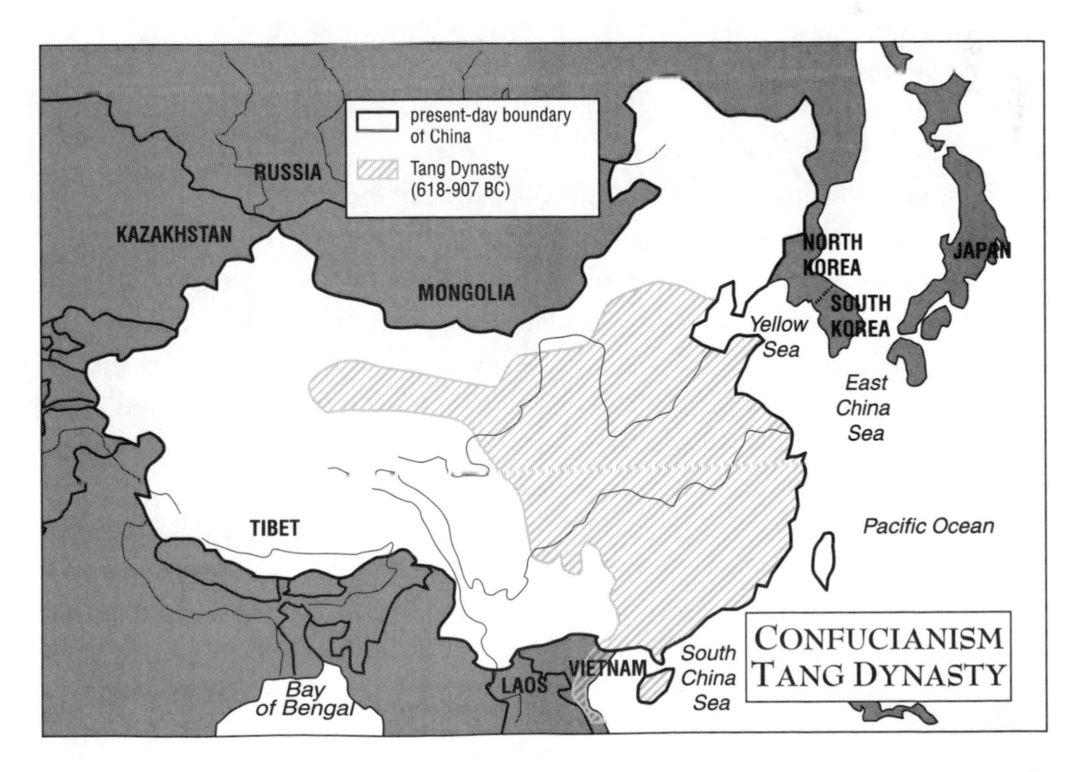

Confucianism
Tang Dynasty

scholars agree that the cult of Confucius did not involve the worship of Confucius as a god. Rather, as Julia Ching explains, the cult's purpose was to honor Confucius as the scholarly ancestor of the entire Chinese nation—the "teacher *par excellence*"—or as the inscription above the altar of the Confucian temples read, "The Teacher of the Ten Thousand Generations."[49]

Confucianism made important gains during the Tang era, firmly reestablishing itself in the nation's bureaucracy and attaining unprecedented imperial support for the cult that had first developed under the Han to venerate the Master.

Confucius Becomes a Legend

As the cult of Confucius was taking root during the Han and Tang dynasties, fantastic legends and myths were developing about the Master's life. The following excerpt from a legend of the period regarding Confucius's birth is taken from Sources of Chinese Tradition, *edited by Wm. Theodore de Bary.*

> The night Confucius was born two azure dragons came down from the heavens and coiled about [his mother's] room. When she had given birth to Confucius as her dream had said, two goddesses appeared in the sky bearing fragrant dew with which they bathed her. The Emperor of Heaven came down and performed the Music of Heavenly Tranquillity. . . . A voice spoke, saying: 'Heaven is moved and gives birth to this sage child. Therefore I have descended and celebrate it with music,' and the sound of the pipes and bells was unlike any heard in this world. . . . Before Confucius was born there was a unicorn which spat up a jade document before some people in Confucius' village . . . and on it was written: 'In the decline of the [Zhou] the descendant of the spirit of water shall be an uncrowned king. . . . A physiognomist [someone who studies the face as an index to character] examined Confucius and said: 'This child is descended from King T'ang of the Yin dynasty. He shall become an uncrowned king under the power of the agent water and, as the scion of kings, attain the highest reverence.'

During the Tang dynasty Confucianism rebounded in China with the construction of temples, such as the one depicted in this illustration, in every province as decreed by Emperor Taizong to honor its ideals.

Yet it would be under China's next dynasties, the Song, the Ming, and the Qing, that the country would become thoroughly Confucianized, with nearly every aspect of its life from politics to social etiquette, ethics to education, guided by Confucian teachings and ideals.

chapter | four

The Apex of Confucianism: Confucianism in China and East Asia from the Tenth to the Twentieth Centuries

From the founding of the Song dynasty in the late tenth century to the fall of the Qing dynasty in the early twentieth century, Confucianism was at the apex of its power and influence in China. During those ten centuries, Confucianism dominated almost every aspect of Chinese thought and life. It was also during this period that Confucianism put down deep roots in Korea, Japan, and

Vietnam, where it would exert a vital influence on the governments, cultures, and societies of those countries.

Neo-Confucianism: Confucianism's Hold over China's Intellectual Life Deepens

By the final century of Tang rule, the influence of Daoism and Buddhism in Chinese political life was steadily eroding in the face of growing Confucian power within the national bureaucracy. The early Tang emperors' commitment to supporting all three of China's main belief systems had been all but forgotten. During the last decades of the Tang era, the emperor, acting under the advice of Confucian advisers, even went so far as to confiscate property belonging to the Buddhists, whom he accused of draining off too much of China's wealth to support their many nuns and monks.

Although Buddhism and Daoism suffered serious political setbacks at the end of the Tang period, they were not totally eclipsed by Confucianism, for the two religions still enjoyed a following among the country's lower class. Of more concern to Confucian scholars and officials than the religious inclinations of their nation's humblest and least-educated inhabitants, however, was the attraction Buddhism and Daoism continued to hold for a number of China's intellectuals. Determined to increase Confucianism's appeal among China's scholarly elite, a remarkable band of Confucian thinkers set out to revitalize their philosophical tradition during the Song era. In the process, they significantly strengthened Confucianism at the expense of its rivals, restoring it to the dominant position it had held in Chinese intellectual life under the Han. During the second century of the Song dynasty, this reform movement gained a name—the School of Principle, or Neo-Confucianism as it is known in the West—as well as an able synthesizer and promoter, the scholar and writer Zhu Xi.

At the heart of the Neo-Confucian movement was a desire to develop the Master's teachings into a more complete school of thought, one capable of answering fundamental questions regarding the structure of the universe and man's destiny in it—the sort of questions that both Buddhism and Daoism addressed, but which Confucius had all but ignored. In effect, the Neo-Confucians hoped to co-opt much of Buddhism's and Daoism's appeal for China's intellectuals by bringing to their philosophy the same kind of systematic explanation of the universe and humankind's place within it that their rivals had already provided.

During the twelfth century, the writer Zhu Xi put together a skillful synthesis of Neo-Confucian ideas regarding the universe and human life that would gain the movement many followers in China. Zhu Xi's modified Confucianism centered on two concepts: "principle," or li, and "material force," or qi. Although the li associated with Confucius's teachings (ritual and etiquette) and the li associated with Neo-Confucianism are pronounced in the same way, they are written in Chinese using different characters to reflect their very different meanings. For Zhu Xi, li was an invisible principle that humans and every created thing possessed. It was unchanging, eternal, and good. As the modern scholar Xinzhong Yao explains, Neo-Confucians viewed principle as the fundamental "pattern of the world . . . that by which the world comes into being and that by which the world runs its course."[50] Material force, on the other hand, was the physical part of the universe and humankind's makeup. It could be changed and even destroyed. According to Zhu Xi, since each person's mind and the mind of the universe are one, human beings are capable of looking through materi-

Wang Yangming: An Important Neo-Confucian Thinker

Neo-Confucianism developed a number of different schools, or interpretations, in China. After Zhu Xi's School of Principle, the most important of these was the School of the Mind. Its best-known exponent was the sixteenth-century philosopher Wang Yangming. Influenced by Buddhism, Wang Yangming emphasized cultivating intuitive knowledge through meditating and thinking, and minimized the importance of studying the Confucian canon. He also taught that principle alone is ultimately real. He did not dispute the reality of material things, but stressed that it is only through reason—in other words, the mind—that a person becomes aware of these things. Although he had many followers, Wang Yangming's interpretation of Neo-Confucianism was never as influential as Zhu Xi's in Chinese thought.

al force to discern the ultimate pattern or li underlying all that exists. Indeed, not only are people capable of perceiving this eternal blueprint within all things, it is their sacred duty to do so. For once people truly understand li, Zhu Xi asserted, that knowledge would guide them in all their relationships and actions, enabling them to achieve harmony with one another and the universe.

Neo-Confucianism teaches that the ability to comprehend the principle behind all of creation rests on two things: first, moral cultivation, meaning adherence to the Con-fucian virtues—especially ren or human-heartedness—and second, an in-depth study of the classic Con-fucian texts. According to Zhu Xi, the most important Confucian texts for understanding the nature of principle consisted of four works. These "Four Books," as they soon came to be known throughout China, included the *Analects,* the *Book of Mencius,* and two shorter works entitled the *Great Learning* and the *Doctrine of the Mean*. Probably dating from the late Zhou and early Han dynasties, the *Great Learning* and the *Doctrine of the Mean* focus on cultivating moral character through overcoming selfish desires and feelings.

A bronze statuette of Confucius, dating from the Qing dynasty in China.

The Neo-Confucian interpretation of the Master's teachings would reign supreme in Chinese thought through all the dynasties that succeeded the Song: the Yuan (1271–1368), the Ming (1368–1644), and the Qing (1644–1911). Although some of China's finest scholars still studied Buddhism and Daoism during these centuries, most of the country's intellectuals embraced Neo-Confucianism, a testament to the skill of Zhu Xi and the other Neo-Confucian philosophers in formulating a sophisticated and comprehensive explanation of the universe to complement the Master's moral, political, and social ideas.

Confucianism's Hold over China's Educational and Political Systems Deepens

From the end of the Song dynasty on, Confucianism, in its revitalized Neo-Confucian form, became more deeply entrenched than ever in Chinese education as the civil service examinations which the educational system served became increasingly focused on the Confucian canon. By the early fourteenth century, aspiring governmental officials not only had to answer detailed questions on the Five Classics, but were also expected to write out large portions of the Four Books and Zhu Xi's commentaries on them from memory. Civil service candidates felt compelled to devote more years than ever before to studying the Confucian texts before attempting to tackle the rigorous tests. Would-be officials now

The *Great Learning* and the *Doctrine of the Mean*

Along with the *Analects* and the *Book of Mencius,* the *Great Learning* and the *Doctrine of the Mean* made up the Four Books—the central focus of all state examinations from the fourteenth to the twentieth centuries. Originally a chapter in the *Book of Rites,* the *Great Learning* includes the sayings of Confucius on the "eight steps"—investigating "things," rectifying the mind, extending knowledge, creating a sincere will, cultivating the self, ordering the family, ordering the state, and bringing harmony and peace to the world. The *Doctrine of the Mean,* which was also originally a chapter in the *Book of Rites,* emphasizes harmony and equilibrium within the self and the universe and the ideal of perfect sincerity or truth. It teaches that to develop their inborn nature and bring themselves into accord with the universe, people must be completely sincere. Those who are able to achieve perfect sincerity within themselves should then help others to cultivate their nature and experience a harmonious union with the universe.

typically began their Confucian studies in elementary school, often continuing with them until they were in their late twenties or even their thirties.

Yet as taxing as the revised Confucian examinations were, those who mastered them could expect to be well rewarded for their trouble. From the Song dynasty through the Qing, virtually the only way for a man to achieve political power and the high social status that went with it was through success on the tests. Consequently, public life at all levels in the empire—local, provincial, and national—was dominated by scholar-officials (or Mandarins as they came to be known in the West) thoroughly grounded in Confucian learning and values. Dynasties rose and fell, but through it all, the Confucian scholar-bureaucrats held on tenaciously to their power and influence. "So long as education and the state examinations were controlled by Confucian scholars and the Confucian Classics remained

Two Chinese civil servants (left) confer with their superiors. Civil servants were required to master Confucian doctrine.

the principal subject of study and examination," D. Howard Smith explains, "Confucianism remained in an impregnable position."[51]

The Confucian scholar-officials further enhanced their authority and prestige within the country through their key role in China's traditional state religious rites—rites widely believed to be essential for the welfare of the whole empire. Of the six central ministries created in imperial China to assist the emperor, unquestionably the most important was the Board of Rites. Like all the other ministries, it was dominated by Confucians from the Song dynasty through the end of the Qing dynasty. The main duty of the Board of Rites was overseeing the highly complex state religious ceremonies that had first developed under the ancient Shang and Zhou dynasties. This was an awesome responsibility, for the assumption was that if these rituals were carried out in strict accordance with Heaven's decrees, harmony would be attained among the human, natural, and spiritual worlds, and the empire and all its inhabitants would prosper.

Chief among the various state religious rites that the Confucian ritual specialists supervised was the annual sacrifice to Heaven at the winter solstice, the shortest day of the year. This elaborate ceremony had to be performed by the emperor himself in his traditional role as the Son of Heaven, the divinely appointed intermediary between humankind and Heaven. It took a veritable legion of Confucian advisers to help the emperor carry out the rites of the cult of Heaven properly. Using the Confucian classic, the *Book of Rites*, as their guide, the Confucian scholar-officials advised their sovereign on every minute detail of the ceremony, from the nature of the sacrifices to be offered, to the robes and gems to be worn, to the music and dances to be performed.

The Confucian scholar-officials also closely assisted the emperor in performing the other so-called "Great Sacrifices" of China's traditional state religion—the sacrifices in honor of the imperial ancestors at the beginnings of the four seasons and the end of the year, the annual sacrifice to Earth at the summer solstice, and the spring and autumn sacrifices to the spirits of Land and Grain. Confucian advisers guided the emperor in carrying out lesser rites in honor of the sun and the moon and numerous spirits of the sky and Earth as well. Unlike the four "Great" sacrifices, these "Medium" and "Small" sacrifices did not have to be executed by the emperor

Worshipers offer a sacrifice at a Confucian temple during a sacred period called Harvest Moon.

himself, however. Consequently, he often delegated them to Confucian scholar-officials in the imperial capital and in provincial and county seats around China, who carried out the sacrifices and other religious rites as another part of their professional duties.

From the Song through the Qing dynasties, Confucianism's religious importance within the Chinese empire was further reinforced by the growing scale and lavishness of the official sacrifices offered to Confucius himself and by the many new temples erected in his honor. "In every city and school where the literati [Confucian scholar-officials] congregate," noted a European visitor to China in the seventeenth century, "there is a very sumptuous temple of Confucius in which . . . every new moon and full moon, and four times in the year, the literati offer to him a certain kind of sacrifice."[52] During the late imperial era, the most elaborate of all the ceremonies in honor of Confucius were performed at the stately Temple of Confucius in Peking and at the even more magnificent temple erected to Confucius in his hometown of

Qufu. Since Confucius particularly loved music, the ceremonies held for him in these great temples featured traditional instrumental and choral music as well as rows of meticulously trained and costumed dancers, the burning of incense, sacrifices including oxen and other animals, and offerings of vegetables and fruits, silk, and jade.

Confucianism and the Rituals of Everyday Life: The Confucianization of Society

Just as Confucianism took on an increasingly critical role in the formal religious rituals of the Chinese state from the Song through the Qing dynasties, during the same period it also exerted more influence than ever on the everyday rituals of the Chinese people. The Master had stressed the importance of adhering to traditional rituals and decorum for people from all levels of society. Thus the Confucian classic, the *Book of Rites,* includes detailed instructions not only for performing the great state rites but also for carrying out the so-called family rituals, such as coming-of-age, marriage, and burial rites. So influential was the *Book of Rites* in shaping Chinese social practices from the Han era—when it was first compiled—until the modern era, that Julia Ching calls it "the backbone of Chinese society."[53] During the Song era, advances in printing

Temples such as this one in China's Shandong province provide worshipers a place to honor Confucian principles.

made the *Book of Rites* more widely available than ever before in China. And by the fourteenth century, the *Book of Rites* had been supplemented by another manual on ritual and decorum by the Neo-Confucian philo-sopher Zhu Xi. Written in the language of the common person, Zhu Xi's extremely popular manual no doubt contributed to Confucianism's increasing importance in guiding the everyday manners and rituals of the Chinese people.

Among the family rituals outlined in the *Book of Rites* and Zhu Xi's manual were ceremonies designed to mark a child's passage into young adulthood. In these coming-of-age, or "capping," ceremonies, teenaged girls received a hairpin, a woman's cap, and a formal adult name, and teenaged boys were given a man's cap and long robe along with their adult name. Boys were also officially presented to their deceased relatives in special ceremonies held at the ancestral shrine after the capping ritual.

In the Confucian texts on ritual, all major family rituals from cappings to marriages to funerals were closely tied to the traditional Chinese ancestral cult, which Confucius had so strongly emphasized in his teachings. Readers were advised to give regular reports to the invisible ancestors on important family events and were provided with guidelines for venerating deceased relatives using special sacrifices and prayers. Although China's ancestral cult existed long before Confucius's time, it was originally restricted almost entirely to the nobility. Because of the enormous value that Confucius attached to honoring ancestors, however, during the centuries following his death, the cult came to be practiced by families at all levels of Chinese society. Wealthy families held lavish ceremonies and feasts for their ancestors in specially constructed ancestral temples, and less prosperous families erected simple altars to their deceased relatives in their homes, where wooden tablets engraved with the names of ancestors were kept, incense burned, and food offerings made.

Since family played such a critical role in Confucian thought, marriage rites received a great deal of attention in the *Book of Rites* and in Zhu Xi's manual. The texts depict in meticulous detail every aspect of the rites, from the formal announcement of the marriage to the ancestors, to the wedding ceremony itself, to the banquet held in honor of the bride and groom. The *Book of Rites* even furnished its readers with instructions on how to eat their wedding feast by describing the behavior of a model bride and groom: "They ate together of the same animal, and joined in supping from the cups made of the same melon; thus showing that they now formed one body, were of equal rank, and pledged to mutual affection."[54]

The everyday practice of filial piety, a key Confucian virtue, was also a major focus of the Confucian texts on ritual. And advice on filial piety was directed as much toward adult children as toward youngsters. For example, the *Book of Rites* contains precise directions on how a married couple should act toward the husband's parents, a point of particular interest to most Chinese, since men and women were expected to live in the husband's family home following marriage. Every day upon rising and dressing, the *Book of Rites* advises, the couple should go directly to the rooms of the parents (or parents-in-law) and follow the same morning ritual:

> On getting to where they are, with bated breath and gentle voice, they should ask if their clothes are too warm or too cold, whether they are ill or pained, or uncomfortable in any part; help and support their parents in quitting or entering the apartment. They will ask whether they want anything and then respectfully bring it. All this they

Followers adhered to the Book of Rites *for all rituals, such as this wedding ceremony.*

> will do with an appearance of pleasure to make their parents feel at ease.[55]

Confucianism's Influence Spreads Beyond China

Confucianism's far-reaching influence on the everyday behaviors of ordinary people as well as on government and education was also felt in other East Asian nations outside of China, especially during the Ming dynasty. During the course of the long Ming era, Confucianism became particularly important in three East Asian countries: Korea, Japan, and Vietnam. In all three, Confucianism was originally imported as part of a larger "cultural package" that included China's sophisticated writing system and rich fine arts tradition, as well as its leading philosophic and religious ideas. Yet, as the modern scholars John and Evelyn Berthrong point out, in each of these East Asian countries, "Confucianism was more than just a borrowed morsel of Chinese cultural life; it became an active part in the lives of the Korean, Japanese, and Vietnamese people over the centuries."[56]

Confucianism was first introduced to Korea from China during the late Han dynasty. Its influence on Korean society and government grew slowly at first, for it faced strong competition from two rival belief systems: Buddhism, which came to Korea in the fourth century A.D., and shamanism, the traditional Korean religion that worships spirits of nature through a medium, or shaman.

It was under the country's longest and most powerful dynasty, the Choson (1392–1910), that Confucianism finally triumphed over its competition in Korea. The dynasty's founder, King Song-gye, made Neo-Confucianism Korea's state religion soon after ascending the throne. A great admirer of Chinese culture and thought, Song-gye had established an especially close alliance with the staunchly Confucian leaders of China's current dynasty, the Ming. Song-gye modeled his new kingdom's administrative system after the Ming's Confucian-controlled bureaucracy and adopted a Confucianism-based civil service examination similar to the one that had long been used in China. As in China, the Korean government soon became dominated by scholar-officials steeped in Confucian ideals and learning. Schools were founded throughout the country to train scholar-bureaucrats in the classic Confucian texts, and the best students were honored at the magnificent Confucius Temple in the imperial capital. In addition to studying the Confucian classics, Korean students were also taught other aspects of Chinese culture, including law, literature, and fine arts, all of which the Koreans gradually adapted and modified to fit their preferences and needs. Korean thinkers expanded and refined the ideas of Zhu Xi and other Chinese Neo-Confucians, particularly their theories regarding human nature.

While Korean intellectuals were attracted to the sophisticated philosophical concepts of Neo-Confucianism, the ordinary people of Korea also found much that was appealing in Confucianism. They seemed to be especially attracted to the family rituals and other rites of everyday life that had come to be associated with Confucianism in China over the centuries. Confucian coming-of-age, mourning, and marriage rites were enthusiastically and strictly followed by Korean families, and copies of the *Book of Rites* and Zhu Xi's manual on family rituals could be found in countless homes in the kingdom right up to the twentieth century. The Confucian emphasis on venerating parents and ancestors also held strong appeal for the Korean people, for family and kinship had long held an honored place within Korean society. Even

Confucianism Is Introduced to the Western World

Confucian thought was introduced to the West by Jesuits (members of a Roman Catholic religious order), who first traveled to China in the sixteenth century. During his long stay in China, the Jesuit missionary Matteo Ricci learned the Chinese language and studied the nine books of the Confucian canon (the Five Classics plus the Four Books). In 1687 a Latin version of the *Analects* was published in Paris by the Jesuits. Confucianism soon earned the admiration of many European intellectuals, including Voltaire, the famous writer and philosopher of the French Revolution, who praised its rational and humanistic bent. As quoted in H. G. Creel, *Confucius: The Man and the Myth,* Voltaire wrote of the *Analects:* "I have never found in them anything but the purest morality, without the slightest tinge of charlatanism."

today, writes Julia Ching, Confucian influence on Korean culture "is especially discerned in the Korean emphasis on filial piety, shown also in ritual mourning for the dead—a reason why Koreans have traditionally preferred to wear white (the color of mourning in East Asia), since they were always mourning for some member of the large, extended family."[57]

Another way in which Confucianism influenced Korean culture and society was the effect it had on the role of women. Before Confucian teachings were introduced to Korea, women were given equal inheritance rights with men and were not expected to leave their families after marriage to live in their husband's family home. Confucianism's strong patriarchal emphasis brought a loss in independence and status for many Korean women. Korean women were stripped of their equal inheritance rights, and over time it became customary for them to move in with their spouse's family, in accordance with Confucian traditions in China. A statute was even enacted giving husbands the right to disown their wives for such offenses as showing disrespect for their parents-in-law, failing to bear a son, or being too talkative.

Confucianism Becomes Important in Japan

About four centuries after being imported to Korea, Confucianism was brought to Japan. As in the case of Korea, along with Confucianism came Chinese forms of writing, art, and literature, and Buddhism. Faced with vigorous competition from Buddhism as well as from Shinto, the country's native religion, at first Confucianism put down only shallow roots in Japan.

Not until the era of the Tokugawa Shogunate (1603–1868), more than one thousand years after its introduction to Japan, was Confucianism finally able to seriously challenge its rivals and become a major influence in Japanese thought and life. The Tokugawa Shogunate was founded during one of the most turbulent and violent eras in Japanese history. Starting in the late twelfth century, Japan had been ruled by both an emperor who functioned as its ceremonial leader, and a shogun, or military dictator, who actually ran the government. Under the country's feudalistic political system, shoguns battled almost continuously for supremacy with ambitious local lords and the samurai (elite noble warriors) who served them. In 1603, the bloodshed finally ended when

The temple of Tosho-gu, built in the seventeenth century, was dedicated to Japan's first shogun, Tokugawa Ieyasu.

the nation was united under the control of a powerful group of shoguns named the Tokugawa Shogunate, after the dynasty's founder, Tokugawa Ieyasu.

For more than two centuries, the Tokugawa Shogunate brought peace and stability to Japan. Its rulers also lent their powerful support to Confucian learning, rituals, and ethics, following a precedent begun by Ieyasu. Under the influence of a Confucian-trained adviser, Ieyasu had promoted Neo-Confucian thought and practices as a means of bringing greater unity and stability to his new empire. In time, Neo-Confucianism became the government's official philosophy, although with a decidedly Japanese twist. For instance, in contrast to Confucianism in China (and Korea), Japanese Confucianism emphasized loyalty to the ruler over filial piety as the most crucial of the "Five Relationships" underlying the harmonious society, with devotion to state considered more important than to parents and family. In addition, Japanese Confucians continued the Shinto tradition of treating their emperor as a god, causing them to reject the traditional Confucian belief that Heaven would remove power from a ruling family if they did not behave in a morally or ritually correct fashion. Finally, the most honored men in Japanese society remained the samurai, or noble warriors, rather than the scholar-bureaucrats who formed the apex of Confucian society in China.

During the Tokugawa era, Confucian ethics became closely linked with Japan's elite samurai class, a phenomenon that would help to strengthen Confucianism's prestige and influence in the country. The long period of peace ushered in by Tokugawa Ieyasu meant that the aristocratic samurai had to find another basis for their privileged position in society aside from their military skills. The samurai would discover in Confucianism their new reason for being. By studying Confucian texts as well as military arts and by supporting a strict code of behavior shaped by Confucian ethics, the samurai managed to

Hayashi Razan on the Arts of War and Peace

Razan, adviser to Ieyasu, the first Tokugawa shogun, took as one of his central tasks helping Japan's samurai to become men of peace as well as of war. In the following selection, Razan explains why the samurai should be as proficient in the arts of peace, and particularly Confucian ethics, as they were in the military arts. All excerpts from Razan's writings are from Sources of Japanese Tradition, *edited by Ryusaku Tsunoda, Wm. Theodore de Bary, and Donald Keene.*

Let us consider [the teaching of] the Sage [Confucius] that "to lead an untaught people into war is to throw them away" [*Analects:* 13:30]. Teaching the people is a civil art, but warfare is a military art. Without both of them, the people would be thrown away. . . . To have the arts of peace, but not the arts of war, is to lack courage. To have the arts of war, but not the arts of peace, is to lack wisdom. . . . A man who is dedicated and has a mission to perform is called a samurai. A man who is of inner worth and upright conduct, who has moral principles and mastery of the arts, is also called a samurai. A man who pursued learning, too, is called a samurai. . . . The *Book of Odes* [the Confucian classic also known as the *Book of Poetry*] says: "Mighty in peace and war is Chi-fu/A pattern to all the peoples." How can a man discharge the duties of his rank and position without combining the peaceful and military arts?

reinvent themselves as Confucian junzi warriors.

The first samurai to apply Confucian moral teachings to the samurai's ethical code was the warrior-scholar Yamaga Soko. In his widely read treatise, *The Way of the Samurai,* Yamaga set forth a formal moral code for samurai that was firmly grounded in Confucian virtues such as loyalty, courage, honesty, and wisdom. Comparing the samurai to Confucius's ideal of the junzi, or noble-minded one, Yamaga argued that the samurai's key peacetime responsibility was to provide a moral example for the ordinary people to follow. "The three classes of the common people [farmers, artisans, and merchants] make him their teacher and respect him," Yamaga wrote of the samurai in the warrior's new role as moral instructor for the nation. And through the samurai's modeling of Confucian virtues, Yamaga concluded, the people "are enabled to understand what is fundamental and what is secondary."[58]

Although Buddhist and Shinto religious practices remained popular among the Japanese masses, Confucianism also gained influence outside of the samurai class during the Tokugawa period, owing in great measure to the efforts of the writer Kaibara Ekken. In his writings, Ekken brought Neo-Confucian teachings into the homes of the Japanese people in a language they could comprehend. His straightforward explanations of Confucian family rituals and everyday etiquette as well as key Confucian values such as filial piety helped to spread the ideas of the Master and his disciples to a group of people who probably would not otherwise have been exposed to them.

Confucian Influence in Vietnam

Like Korea and Japan, Vietnam adopted much from China's rich culture, from its writing system and art to its Confucian philosophy. For about one thousand years, from the second century B.C. to the tenth century A.D., the area that would eventually be named Vietnam was under direct Chinese control. During the long Chinese occupation and even after Vietnam achieved independence, Chinese and particularly Confucian influence remained strong, especially within the country's bureaucracy and state-supported educational system. A Chinese-style civil service examination system and national

The elite Japanese samurai embraced Confucian principles during the Tokugawa period.

university were created, Confucian shrines built, and an elite Confucian scholar-official class gained power and prestige. It was within this well-educated and privileged class that Confucianism attained its greatest influence in Vietnam—a degree of influence that it was unable to achieve among the country's peasant masses.

Throughout the centuries following its introduction to Vietnam, Confucianism had to compete with Buddhism and other belief systems, including the country's indigenous religious tradition in which a host of spirits and local deities are worshipped. Confucianism's religious rivals remained especially strong among the ordinary people of Vietnam, who also clung stubbornly to traditional Southeast Asian ideas about women and their role, ideas that were decidedly un-Confucian.

To a greater degree than their counterparts in Korea and Japan, the ordinary people of Vietnam seemed determined to pick and choose what they were willing to accept from China's Confucian tradition, which perhaps explains why Confucianism failed to gain as wide or as loyal a following in Vietnam as it did in the other two countries. For example, although the key Confucian value of

The Confucian Temple of Literature was built in Hanoi, Vietnam, in 1070.

filial piety took firm hold among all levels of Vietnamese society, in defiance of Confucian teachings regarding the well-ordered family, lower-class families remained far less patriarchal than those in imperial China, Korea, or Japan. Confucianism taught that a woman's place was in the home, yet Vietnamese women typically worked side by side with men in the fields or as craftspeople or shop owners. Moreover, if a Vietnamese woman was widowed, she was considered free to remarry, an attitude the Chinese found shocking, since the *Book of Rites* specifically forbade widows from remarrying. One Chinese emperor was so dismayed by what he considered to be the Vietnamese women's un-Confucian morals that he sent as a gift to the people of Vietnam ten thousand copies of a Confucian text on proper womanly behavior.

If the Vietnamese were hesitant to embrace all aspects of Confucian teachings and practices, Confucianism nonetheless managed to take deep root within the country's thought and life during the centuries following its introduction from China. During the approximately one-thousand-year period starting with the Song dynasty in China and ending in the early twentieth century, Confucianism reached the peak of its influence not only in Vietnam and other East Asian countries such as Korea and Japan, but also in its homeland. With the dawning of the modern era, however, Confucianism would find itself facing a new and very uncertain future.

chapter | five

From Vilification to Rehabilitation: Confucianism in Twentieth-Century China

During the first decades of the twentieth century, Confucianism experienced a dramatic decline, relinquishing its hold over the political and educational systems of China and the other East Asian countries in which it had been a dominant force for centuries. As East Asia was opened to foreign trade and Western culture began to penetrate the region, age-old Confucian traditions and teachings were denounced by many Chinese intellectual and political leaders as a negative force that had suppressed innovation and progress. Yet, Confucianism was never merely the ideology of an intellectual or political elite. It was also the belief system of countless ordinary men and women. Thus, even as it lost its official status and privileges in China and other East Asian countries, Confucianism remained a potent moral and cultural influence over the lives of millions. And today, Confucianism is also making a remarkable comeback in China and throughout East Asia as the subject of extensive scholarly research and debate.

East Meets West: Confucian China and the Western Powers

Up until the final years of China's last dynasty, the Qing (1644–1911), Confucianism enjoyed unprecedented strength and prestige within its homeland. Although the Manchus who founded the dynasty were a non-Chinese ethnic group, they embraced Chinese culture, and particularly Confucianism, promoting Confucian studies and meticulously carrying out the state rituals traditionally associated with the philosophy. Generally viewed as the source of all wisdom, the Confucian classics dominated every level of schooling during the Qing era. Independent thought and creativity were discouraged within an educational system that focused above all on rote memorization of the Confucian texts and the officially accepted explanations of their meaning. The high value that Qing educators placed on maintaining the status quo bred a profound conservatism and unwillingness to change among the empire's Confucian-trained officials. When Europeans and Americans began making inroads into China in the 1800s, this conservatism, combined with a deep-seated belief that Confucian China was the most advanced civilization on Earth, would make it hard for the Chinese to come to terms with the Westerners' immensely different culture and ideas.

Before the nineteenth century, the West had little impact on China. Convinced that their country had no more need of foreign goods than they did of foreign learning or culture, China's Confucian officials severely limited international commerce, particularly from the mid–eighteenth century on. By the early 1800s, however, many Western governments and traders had become impatient with China's trade restrictions. The British, in particular, wanted silk and tea from China and were determined to find a commodity the Chinese people would be willing to buy in return. They finally hit upon opium, a highly addictive narcotic derived from a type of poppy. Soon Chinese ports were flooded with the dangerous drug. When the Qing emperor responded

In 1842, following a three-year war with the British, China was forced to cede the trading port of Hong Kong.

by prohibiting the sale or use of opium in the empire, the British declared war rather than give up their lucrative new trade. Three years later, in 1842, China was defeated by Britain's more modernized military and compelled to accept a humiliating treaty lifting many trade restrictions and ceding the island of Hong Kong to Britain. During the following decades, Chinese officials were forced to sign a series of what they dubbed "unequal treaties" with other militarily strong Western nations, giving the foreigners sweeping rights to trade, preach their religion, and set up their own courts of law, thereby allowing them to evade the Chinese justice system.

China's feebleness in its dealings with the Western powers made a deep impression on its chief Asian rival, Japan. In 1894, the Japanese invaded Korea, a longtime tributary of China. Within a year, China had suffered a humiliating defeat against Japan's modernized armed forces and renounced all claim to both Korea and the island of Taiwan, which it had controlled since the seventeenth century.

After China's disastrous war with Japan, the Western powers rushed to take advantage of its weakness, demanding and receiving broad new trading concessions as well as naval stations, mining and transportation rights, and any other forms of control over China's economy, land, and natural resources that they could concoct. Many Chinese were infuriated not only with the greedy and arrogant foreigners but also with the Qing rulers and their Confucian advisers, whom they accused of making foolish and cowardly concessions to the Westerners. The most militant of the government's critics formed secret societies devoted to ridding their country of all outsiders. One of these societies, the Boxers, became so powerful that a force of eight foreign nations was required to stop its members from attacking and killing Western traders and missionaries.

The growing violence within their society, combined with China's repeated humiliations at the hands of foreigners, convinced many Chinese that their nation had to change if it was to avoid total collapse. Once confident in the superiority of their Confucian-dominated political and educational systems, they were becoming more and more discouraged by the daunting military strength and technological know-how of the Western powers and their

Japanese forces invaded Korea in 1894.

modernized neighbor, Japan. As the nineteenth century drew to a close, even some of China's Confucian scholar-officials were beginning to wonder if their empire's ancient Confucian system was capable of meeting the overwhelming new challenges facing their country from within and without.

Kang Youwei: Confucian Reformer

For the majority of Chinese, reform was still viewed as occurring within China's existing governmental and educational systems, not as a complete transformation of those systems. Most assumed that the answer to China's problems lay in finding a way to preserve traditional Chinese and Confucian values and culture while taking the best of what the West had to offer, especially in the area of technology.

One Chinese who had definite ideas about the types of reforms that were needed was the Confucian official and scholar Kang Youwei (1858–1927). Kang's reform plan centered on making the Chinese government into a constitutional monarchy similar to the British system, modernizing the educational system by introducing Western technology and science, and strengthening Confucianism's religious role to make it the equivalent of Christianity in the West. To justify his program, Kang claimed that the Master himself had not been merely a transmitter of ancient wisdom but a courageous reformer who sought to better his society and government by making education and moral character instead of noble birth the main qualifications for public office. Kang Youwei, notes Wm. Theodore de Bary, firmly believed that the "way of the sages was to meet change with change; Confucius himself had done so, and if alive today would do so again."[59]

In 1898, China's young new emperor, Guangxu, agreed to implement Kang's program. But it never stood a chance. Guangxu's aunt, the dowager empress, was a staunch conservative who strongly opposed any trifling with China's ancient Confucian tradition. After imprisoning her nephew and seizing control of the government, the dowager empress promptly terminated Kang's reform plan, which had been adopted barely one hundred days before. Over the next decade until her death in 1908, however, popular opinion combined with foreign pressure compelled the empress to enact some limited reforms, including the creation of a more Westernized educational system and army and the abolition of the Confucian-based civil service examination.

Confucianism Under the Chinese Republic

By the time the empress finally realized the necessity for reform, however, it was too late to save not only the Qing dynasty in whose name she ruled, but China's age-old monarchical system as well. During the last years of her life, a group of the government's most ardent opponents banded together to topple the Chinese monarchy once and for all. This diverse coalition included intellectuals and professionals, such as Dr. Sun Yat-sen, who hoped to establish a republic as well as regional military commanders. After six years of fighting, the rebels were triumphant. In 1912 Sun Yat-sen declared the establishment of the Chinese Republic.

Almost from the start, the Republic struggled to survive. Sun Yat-sen was quickly replaced as president by a conservative and power-hungry regional military commander, Yuan Shikai. Yuan secretly dreamed of establishing a new dynasty with himself as emperor. When Yuan's scheme became apparent, Sun Yat-sen and his republican followers founded the Guomindang, or Nationalist Party, and staged a revolt. By the time of Yuan's death in 1916, Sun Yat-sen

Chiang Kai-shek, nationalist leader of the Chinese Republic, promoted Confucianism as a moral code for his country.

had managed to establish a rival nationalist government in southern China, while northern China was falling more and more under the sway of ambitious local warlords. After more than ten years of anarchy and civil war, China was finally united once more under a nationalist government led by Chiang Kai-shek, Sun Yat-sen's successor as head of the Guomindang.

Meanwhile, important changes were taking place in Chinese thought. More and more Chinese, particularly students and young professionals, were blaming Confucianism for what they viewed as their country's humiliating backwardness and weakness in comparison with the Western nations. As John and Evelyn Berthrong explain, Confucianism's young critics reasoned that if the philosophy was the main element of traditional Chinese society and culture, and if China "was so far behind the West in terms of wealth and power, then Confucianism must be to blame for this failure."[60] China's once-revered Confucian legacy was regarded by many of the would-be reformers "as a weight and burden—an intellectual shackle on the mind,"[61] writes Julia Ching. For them, it represented an antiquated tradition that must be swept away in favor of a new Chinese culture molded by Western-style science, technology, and democracy. In time, this intellectual revolution came to be called the May Fourth movement, after a large student demonstration held on May 4, 1919, in Peking. Convinced that Confucianism was preventing China from attaining its rightful place in the modern world, followers of the May Fourth movement adopted "Smashing Confucius's Shop"[62] as their slogan.

Despite the vocal anti-Confucian movement of the 1910s and 1920s, during the early thirties, China's new nationalist leader, Chiang Kai-shek, tried to restore Confucianism to a place of honor in his country's life and thought. Chiang's campaign to revive Confucianism did not entail bringing back the old Confucian-based civil service examinations that had been discarded during the final years of the Qing dynasty. Nor did it involve an effort to revive the formal state religious cult that had been so closely associated with Confucianism during imperial times, but which had fallen out of use soon after the founding of the Republic. Rather, Chiang sought to renew what he believed to be Confucianism's rapidly declining moral influence over Chinese society. Unlike many of the philosophy's youthful critics, Chiang had received a traditional Confucian education and was convinced that Confucian ethics still had a vital role to play in China. Consequently, his pro-Confucian crusade, the New Life movement, stressed the importance of core Confucian values such as courtesy, modesty, honesty, and altruism (unselfish concern for others) for promoting national unity and morale.

Although deeply optimistic regarding the potential of his New Life movement for bettering Chinese

Chiang Kai-shek and the New Life Movement

Convinced that Confucian ethics were essential to the well-being and success of the young Chinese Republic, in 1934 Chiang Kai-shek launched his New Life movement as a national moral reform program, promoting such Confucian virtues as social decorum, righteousness, and honesty. The following quotations from Chiang's Essentials of the New Life Movement *are from* Sources of Chinese Tradition, *edited by Wm. Theodore de Bary.*

The general psychology of our people today can be described as spiritless. What manifests itself in behavior is this: lack of discrimination between good and evil, between what is public and what is private, and between what is primary and what is secondary. . . . If the situation should remain unchanged, it would be impossible even to continue living under such miserable conditions. In order to develop the life of our nation, protect the existence of our society, and improve the livelihood of our people, it is absolutely necessary to wipe out these unwholesome conditions and to start to lead a new and rational life. . . .

The New Life Movement aims at the promotion of a regular life guided by the four virtues, namely li, i, lien, and ch'ih [decorum, righteousness, honesty, and sense of shame]. . . . The four virtues are the essential principles for the promotion of morality. They form the major rules for dealing with men and human affairs, for cultivating oneself, and for adjustment to one's surroundings. Whoever violates these rules is bound to fail; and a nation which neglects them will not survive.

society, Chiang was soon forced to put the program aside in the face of more pressing concerns. During much of the thirties, he and his nationalist regime faced powerful enemies from within and outside China's borders. In 1937, the highly modernized Japanese military invaded China, and within a year, Japan controlled much of the eastern part of the nation. Along with the Japanese threat, Chiang also faced a serious domestic challenge to his rule in the form of a burgeoning Communist movement. Communism is a system of social organization in which the means of producing goods are communally owned, and all members share the labor and the goods generated from that labor. Founded in 1921, by the mid-thirties the Chinese Communist Party had a large army of its own and a wide following among China's landless peasant masses.

Despite being rigorously persecuted by Chiang, the Communist movement grew steadily, especially during World War II (1941–1945 in Asia), when the nationalist government was preoccupied with fighting Japan. In 1949, after three years of full-scale civil war, the Communists finally defeated the Guomindang, forcing Chiang and 1 million of his supporters to flee to Taiwan. There Chiang established a pro-Confucian government (the Republic of China). Back on the mainland, the new Communist-controlled People's Republic of China (PRC) under the leadership of Mao Zedong swiftly replaced Confucianism with Communism as the central ideology of the government and the nation.

Confucianism Under Mao Zedong

Mao and his Communist cohorts were even more stridently anti-Confucian than the leaders of the May Fourth movement had been. Labeling Confucianism as backward-looking and feudalistic, they accused it of bolstering up an aristocratic scholar class that hoarded the privileges of wealth, education, and social prestige, leaving the masses in ignorance and poverty. Furthermore, the Communists charged, Confucianism's strong emphasis on filial piety and a patriarchal family system encouraged inequality between the sexes, relegating Chinese women to a state of perpetual subjugation. The Chinese Communist Party organized huge demonstrations in which effigies of the Sage were burned and Mao declared that he had hated Confucius from the time he was a young boy.

Mao Zedong's Red Guards vandalized many sacred sites dedicated to Confucius.

In 1966, concerned that the Chinese people were losing their revolutionary fervor, Mao founded the Cultural Revolution. Its alleged goal was the creation of the pure socialist citizen. Instead, the decade-long Cultural Revolution became an excuse for vandalism and violence at the hands of Mao's storm troopers, the Red Guards. With Mao's blessing, the young men and women of the Red Guard humiliated and attacked teachers and scholars and declared war on all relics of China's pre-Communist past, including its numerous Daoist and Buddhist temples and monasteries. Confucianism soon became one of the Red Guard's chief targets. Determined to purge any lingering vestiges of the once powerful tradition from Chinese culture and thought, Guards stormed temples and mansions constructed in Confucius's memory and even invaded private homes, carrying off Confucian books and destroying the altars and tablets used in the ancient ancestor cult that had become so closely associated with the Master.

Inevitably, the Red Guards made their way to the most sacred Confucian site in the country—Qufu, the Master's birth and burial place, and the home of the Kong family mansion and majestic Confucius Temple. Calling Qufu "the resting place of the stinking corpse of Confucius,"[63] Mao's young soldiers went on a rampage in the historic city, smashing commemorative columns, statues, and tablets and desecrating the tombs of Confucius and his descendants—the supreme expression of contempt according to Chinese custom. After the Red Guards departed Qufu, however, something remarkable happened. The people of the town quietly gathered up the stone fragments that had once made up the monument marking the Master's grave and hid them in their homes, all the time knowing that they risked imprisonment—or worse—if caught. It seemed as though China's ancient Confucian heritage was not going to be as easy to destroy as Mao had imagined.

Confucianism and the Communist Government After Mao

In 1976 the Cultural Revolution finally died along with its by now elderly creator, Mao Zedong. Mao's successors were far more interested in carrying out economic reforms than in eradicating Confucianism and other remnants of China's pre-Communist past from their nation. Beginning in the late 1970s, the Communist government embarked on an ambitious program to modernize the PRC and rebuild its ailing economy. Education was seen as a vital part of this program, and after the humiliations and persecutions of the Mao years, scholars and teachers regained their place of honor in Chinese society. "The spirit of learning so important in Confucianism is once again being encouraged and fostered as China strives to modernize rapidly,"[64] notes scholar Julian Pas.

During the 1980s, Confucianism gradually won acceptance from the Communist regime as an important component of China's rich cultural heritage, which was now being viewed not as a threat to the Communist way of life, but as a vital means of bolstering national morale and unity. As the Communist leadership increasingly linked national

Chinese youths let out a cheer for their leader, Chairman Mao Zedong.

pride to the many accomplishments of China's long civilization, the Confucian legacy became something to be preserved and honored, not destroyed. By the end of the decade, the head of the Communist Party and future president of the PRC, Jiang Zemin, was publicly praising Confucius as "one of China's great thinkers" and an integral part of "our fine national tradition."[65]

Yet, though Confucius has been thoroughly rehabilitated in recent years by China's Communist leadership, officials are careful to make clear that no matter what role Confucianism might have played in imperial China, it is not to be viewed in any way, shape, or manner as a religion today. As far as Chinese Communist policy is concerned, notes the scholar J. R. Levenson, "Confucianism as a religion is a dead issue."[66] It would appear that this stance is rooted in orthodox Communist ideology, which teach-

The Historic Confucius Temple at Qufu

In The Turning of the Tide *(edited by Julian Pas), Paula Swart and Barry Till describe the world's largest Confucian shrine, the Confucius Temple at Qufu, China:*

According to one tradition, the Confucian temple in Qufu was originally constructed in 478 B.C. by Duke Ai of the state of Lu, a year after Confucius' death. Over the centuries it has been rebuilt and enlarged, so that most present buildings of the large complex date from the Ming and Qing Dynasties. At one time the temple occupied one fifth of Qufu's total area and owned several hectares of land which were used for the sole purpose of raising the large number of pigs, sheep and cattle required for the seasonal sacrifices. Instead of burning cheap paper effigies, the worshippers performed the full sacrificial rites laid down in the books of old. The temple, one of the architectural marvels of China, looks like an imperial palace with magnificent yellow-tile buildings within a surrounding red wall and with nine interior gates opening to individual courtyards set off by stretches of ancient pines and cypresses.

es that religion has no legitimate place or function in society and should therefore be discouraged.

Discounting Confucianism as a religion leaves the Communist government with much more leeway to promote Confucian scholarship. During the past two decades, it has generously supported the study of China's Confucian past, including its rituals, classic writings, and relationship to traditional music and art. Translations of the Confucian canon in the simplified language of the people have been encouraged and scores of scholarly books and theses on Confucianism published. In 1985 the Association for Research on Confucius was founded with the government's blessing. Since then, it has sponsored numerous academic symposiums and other activities related to the Master and his teachings.

The Restoration of Qufu

Nowhere in the People's Republic of China is Confucianism's new post-Mao status as conspicuous as in Confucius's birthplace of Qufu in modern-day Shandong province. During the 1980s, the Chinese government began pouring millions of dollars into the city to repair the temples, mansions, shrines, tombs, and other historic structures vandalized by Mao's Red Guards. They were aided in their work by those courageous townspeople who had hidden away the fragments of Confucius's demolished tomb monument years earlier. In the late nineties, work was begun in the city on an impressive new conference and research center dedicated to Confucian scholarship.

For nearly two decades, a memorial ceremony has also been held for Confucius each September 28 (the traditional date of his birthday) in Qufu's renovated Confucius Temple. The elaborate ceremony includes readings from the *Analects*, ancient music, and silk-robed dancers performing intricate steps dating from Confucius's own time. Confucius's descendants, many of whom remained in Qufu, are given seats of honor at the birthday celebrations, which are well attended by Chinese and foreign tourists alike. In keeping with the government's official stance, the ceremonies are not designed to be religious in any way; rather, it is their historical value that is emphasized. Significantly, the rites are not performed by high government officials as they would have been during China's imperial age. Instead, they are carried out by hired opera performers.

Extensive renovation has restored Confucius Temple in Qufu, birthplace of Confucius.

Confucianism's Continuing Influence over Everyday Life in China

Throughout the dramatic ups and downs Confucianism experienced among China's ruling elite during the course of the twentieth century, from its nadir under Mao Zedong to its new respectability under President Jiang Zemin, the ancient philosophy quietly lived on in the hearts and minds of many of the country's citizens. Above all, Confucianism lived on in Chinese attitudes toward family. Although Mao attempted to replace the traditional Confucian loyalty to family with loyalty to the state, the Confucian ideal of family was too deeply ingrained in Chinese life to be easily abandoned. Today, especially in the rural areas where most Chinese reside, daily life continues to revolve around the family, just as it did when Confucianism was China's official ideology. The Confucian value of filial piety also survives in Communist China. Parents are typically treated with deep respect by their children, and most adult Chinese feel a strong obligation to care for their elderly relations. This traditional attitude actually pleases the current Communist leadership, reports Julian Pas, since it greatly eases "the financial burden on the state as regards social security costs."[67]

Continued loyalty to Confucian values in the PRC is also evident in contemporary marriage customs. Although the government supports freedom of choice in marriage, most young people still seek their parents' approval before selecting a marital partner. Yet if marriage customs have not changed substantially since the Communist takeover, attitudes toward women have been vastly transformed. The Confucian view of women was that their proper place was at home, caring for their husbands and children. Under Communist rule, however, all adults, male and female alike, are expected to work outside the home. And although the top leadership of the PRC is still dominated by men, women have achieved a degree of respect and independence in Communist society they were not afforded in the Confucian era.

Some of the core family rituals associated with Confucianism even managed to survive Mao's virulent anti-Confucian crusade. In remoter rural areas, many of the traditional practices of the ancestral cult promoted by Confucius never disappeared, even during the height of the Cultural Revolution. Today, under a more tolerant regime, ancestral altars and tablets are reappearing in private homes in larger towns and cities throughout China as well. Yet the age-old ancestral

Celebrants dressed in traditional robes commemorate the birthday of Confucius at the Confucius Temple in Qufu.

practices are being forced to adapt to a new era. In response to China's grave overpopulation problem, in the late 1970s the Communist government mandated that married couples could have only one child each, meaning that countless families will have no male descendant to carry out the customary ancestral rites. Either daughters will have to be entrusted with performing the ancestral rituals, marking a signifi-

Confucianism Outside of China in the Twentieth Century

Outside of China, Confucianism also experienced times of great strength as well as profound weakness during the course of the twentieth century. The fortunes of Confucianism varied in the different countries of East Asia in the modern era. In Vietnam, Confucianism reached the peak of its influence under the country's last ruling family, the Nguyens, then began a steady downward spiral after the country became a French colony in the late 1800s through its long civil war between the Communist North and U.S.-backed South until the Communist triumph in 1975. In Korea, Confucianism was disestablished in the early twentieth century with the fall of the Choson dynasty and the traditional Korean state, yet retained much of its influence over Korean social attitudes and practices.

In Japan, Confucianism, with its emphasis on traditional learning and rituals, was largely neglected in the late nineteenth and early twentieth centuries when the nation was rapidly modernizing. Later, however, and especially from the 1930s until the end of World War II, the Japanese government promoted Confucian values such as loyalty and filial piety to encourage obedience to the state and social stability. Following Japan's defeat in 1945, the Japanese again turned their backs on Confucianism, which had become closely tied in many minds with the nation's deposed leaders. Yet, as Japan rebuilt itself as one of the world's leading economic powers during the final decades of the century, Japanese Confucianism underwent another sea change, reemerging as an important force in the national educational system and the topic of intense scholarly study and debate.

cant break with Confucian tradition, or the rites will have to be abandoned altogether in many households.

Although Confucianism lost its preeminent position in China's government administration and educational system during the early years of the twentieth century, at the beginning of the twenty-first century, it is evident that Confucianism still retains much of its moral and cultural influence over the lives of China's people. Whether it will be able to hold on to that influence, or perhaps even expand it, in the century ahead is a question for which there are no ready answers.

chapter | six

The Relevance of Confucianism Today

What will be the role of Confucianism in the twenty-first century? Will it survive as a vibrant and influential system of belief or will it be little more than a museum piece, a remnant of East Asia's past? In our rapidly changing world, can a two-thousand-year-old philosophy still make a meaningful contribution to the quality of people's personal lives and to society as a whole? And what specifically is the relevance of Confucianism—if any—for its birthplace, for the rest of East Asia, and for the West in the century ahead? In recent years, these questions and others regarding Confucianism's significance for the modern world have generated intense debate, with a host of economists, social commentators, and politicians from all parts of the globe putting forth some very different answers.

Confucianism's Relevance to the Challenges Facing the PRC

As it has so many times before in the course of its long history, China confronts tremendous challenges in a changing world. The People's Republic of China is in the midst of an economic boom of unprecedented proportions. Yet as China's economy takes off, the country faces a host of problems including overpopulation, serious pollution, and an overburdened infrastructure, with transportation, banking, power, and communications systems strained to their limits. China's social stability is also being threatened by the growing gap between rich and poor, a consequence of the new market-oriented economic policies adopted by the Communist leadership in the late 1980s. In addition, as China has undergone economic reform and become increasingly open to the rest of the world, demands for political freedom have grown, as witnessed in the mass demonstrations for democracy held in Tiananmen Square in 1989.

Many contemporary observers believe that in addition to the economic, political, and environmental problems besetting the nation, China is suffering from a moral and ideological crisis of enormous proportions. Willem Van Kemenade, a journalist who has lived and worked in the PRC for many years, is convinced that as the PRC moves toward a market economy, its official ideology of Communism is becoming increasingly irrelevant. China, he writes, has become little more than "'a pile of loose sand' without cohesion." The country is confronting an identity crisis, Van Kemenade believes, with the "search for new values, ideas, theories, and systems that could restore

Demonstrators seeking greater personal and political freedoms crowd into Tiananmen Square May 4, 1989.

order and morality becoming more urgent every day."[68]

Some social commentators, including Van Kemenade, view Confucianism as the answer to China's alleged ideological and ethical void. They assert that Confucius's ancient teachings regarding the virtuous individual and the harmonious society hold more relevance today for China and its people than ever before. Confucianism, they maintain, can provide the moral focus and social cohesion that contemporary China seems to lack. "The needs of the present era are order, discipline, morality, and education, all of which are basic themes of Confucianism,"[69] contends Van Kemenade.

Over the past two decades, the PRC's leadership has also embraced the idea that Confucianism has social and moral relevance for present-day China, at least as a strictly secular (nonreligious) system of thought. Since it promotes harmony in social relationships and respect for authority within the family and state, as well as such virtues as honesty, decorum, and generosity, Confucianism is perceived by its Communist proponents as a force for stability in a rapidly changing society. However, the Communist leadership does not support the traditional Confucian conception of the orderly family as being strongly patriarchal. From the time of Mao Zedong on, the PRC's leaders have been outspoken in their disdain for the Confucian ideal of the virtuous woman as being submissive to the men in her life and completely tied to family and domestic obligations. The Communist administration prides itself on supporting equal educational and employment opportunities for women, although women are still far from achieving equal representation in China's male-dominated government.

At a national conference honoring Confucius's birthday in 1994, the keynote speaker and vice premier of the PRC, Li Lanqing, spoke at length about the vital importance of teaching Confucian values such as self-discipline, loyalty, and harmony to the nation's rising generation. Regarding Confucianism's relevance to the challenges and opportunities currently facing China, and particularly its youth, the vice premier had this to say: "Under the present social conditions in a developing market economy with increased commodity production, Confucianism provides rich material for the fostering of a new, idealistic, moral, and disciplined generation. . . . The Confucius of China's traditional culture will shine with new life in the new century and make new contribu-

Many people in contemporary China still follow Confucian principles.

tions to the continuing development of human society."[70]

Not all Chinese who admire Confucianism and believe its teachings are still relevant are happy with the official government campaign to promote Confucian ethics, however. Journalist and longtime resident of China Linda Jakobson writes of meeting a professor of philosophy in Beijing in the late 1990s who was highly skeptical of the Communists' motives in supporting Confucian ethics and concerned about the potentially harmful influence of their pro-Confucian crusade. During Mao Zedong's regime, this same professor had been sentenced to several years of hard labor for defending Confucius's teachings as "progressive" in an academic paper. "Now they are hysterically attempting to find something to counterbalance the overemphasis on materialism" in Chinese society, he told Jakobson regarding pro-Confucian officials such as Li Lanqing. "As a result, the teachings of Confucius have become even more blurred, even among intellectuals. . . . The leaders are simply picking out thoughts to suit their needs, as if plucking flowers for a floral arrangement they had designed ahead-of-time."[71] The government's selective and self-serving reinterpretation of the Master, some Chinese worry, is giving the rising generation a distorted view of his teachings—a view that stresses the citizens' duties to their rulers while ignoring the leaders' obligations to their people, particularly that of placing the public welfare first.

The Relevance of Confucianism to the World: The East Asian Economic Miracle

The issue of whether Confucian teachings have any relevance to the needs and concerns of contemporary China has drawn a great deal of attention in recent years. So, too, has the question of their potential usefulness for the human community as a whole. Many people, Asian and Western alike, agree that Confucian practices and ideals have deep significance for the opportunities and challenges facing people around the world today. Where they differ, however, is in their conceptions of the exact nature of that significance, whether economic, social, or political.

Over the past twenty years or so, a number of leading scholars and commentators have focused their attention on the economic relevance of Confucianism to the modern world. Confucian values, they contend, can promote economic success. To bolster their argument, these scholars point to the so-called East Asian economic miracle of the post–World War II era. The "East Asian economic miracle" refers to the astounding rate of growth experienced by the economies of Japan, South Korea, Taiwan, Singapore, and Hong Kong (now part of the PRC) during the decades immediately following World War II. Even the economic downturns suffered in some of these countries during the late 1990s and early twenty-first century fade in comparison with the overall dynamic economic character of their small corner of the globe. When economists analyzed what it was that these five prosperous East Asian countries had in common, they realized that all shared a strong Confucian heritage. In Japan and South Korea, where the philosophy had been imported centuries earlier

Confucianism and the East Asian "Economic Miracle"

Gilbert Rozman, a Princeton University historian, is one of the leading advocates of the theory that the Confucian ethic fueled East Asia's so-called economic miracle in the late twentieth century. According to Rozman, quoted in T. R. Reid, Confucius Lives Next Door*:*

> "This-worldly" in its orientation, Confucianism teaches individuals of both high and low birth to strive for success in their lifetime and in the long-term interests of their direct descendants. One need not reconcile oneself to one's current lot in life, it says. . . . Education is for everyone. Moral cultivation can be expected to pay rich dividends.
>
> In this environment, families could anticipate that hard work, savings, study, and attention to market opportunities would improve their standing in society. Such circumstances fostered a competitive and, within understandable premodern limitations, an entrepreneurial spirit.

from China, and in Taiwan, Singapore, and Hong Kong with their primarily ethnic Chinese populations, Confucianism, although no longer the state ideology, remained a vital moral and social influence.

In attempting to pinpoint Confucianism's significance for the East Asian economic boom, scholars singled out a number of core Confucian values. These included respect for education, a strong work ethic, frugality, self-discipline, responsibility, a shared sense of loyalty and obligation between superior and subordinate members in relationships, including the manager-employee relationship, and a willingness to cooperate with others to further the common good. Countries in other parts of the world could prosper as well, some scholars concluded, if their citizens would only follow the East Asian example and practice the traditional Confucian values within their schools, workplaces, and homes.

Other scholars and commentators, however, are skeptical regarding Confucianism's usefulness for promoting economic prosperity in East Asia or elsewhere in the globe.

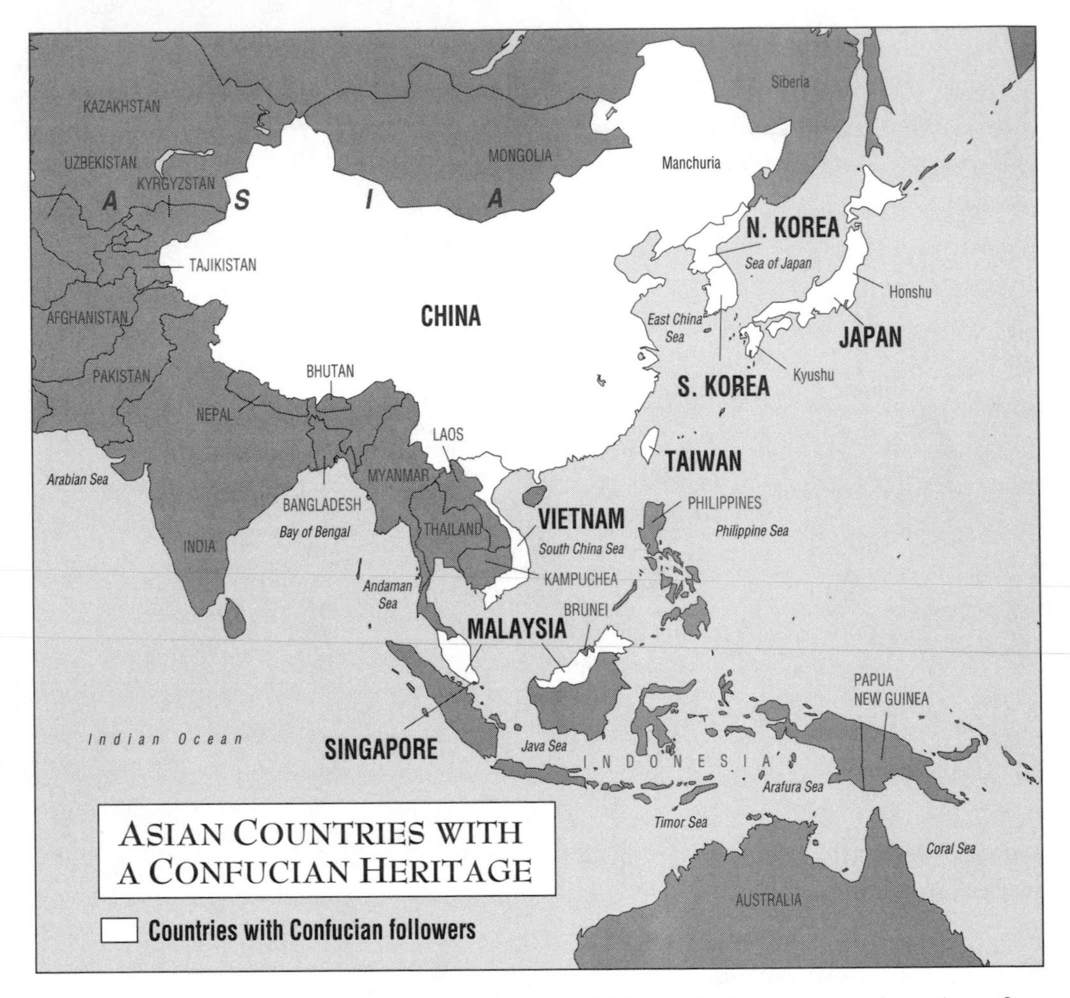

ASIAN COUNTRIES WITH A CONFUCIAN HERITAGE

"As for the relationship between Asian values [i.e., Confucian values] and economic success, that is dubious at best," writes Francis Fukuyama, a professor of public policy. For most of the first half of the twentieth century, he notes, "Asia as a whole was rightly regarded as an economic basket-case."[72] Other scholars agree with Fukuyama, pointing out that the great economic growth in the Confucianized nations of East Asia occurred only after their adoption of Western technology and Western styles of business and economic organization following World War II. Moreover, they point out, the Confucian scholar-officials who stood at the apex of traditional Confucian societies looked down on trade and technical skills, making Confucianism a serious hindrance to East Asia's economic development for centuries.

The Relevance of Confucianism to the Modern World: The East Asian Social Miracle

While some people have stressed the relevance of Confucianism for promoting economic success in the modern world, others have emphasized its potential social benefits. American journalist T. R. Reid, a resident of Japan for many years, believes that what has been referred to as East Asia's "social miracle"—its comparatively low rates of illegitimacy, divorce, drug use, theft, vandalism, and violent crime—is a direct result of the region's Confucian heritage. In Japan, Taiwan, South Korea, and Singapore, he notes, people are continually reminded of Confucian values such as loyalty, compassion, politeness, and responsibility at the workplace, at school, and even while waiting for a train or driving on the highway. Just about anywhere one goes in these nations, says Reid, one will "find moral instruction right before your eyes—often in letters (or characters) ten feet tall . . . these countries are constantly preaching values, morality, and good citizenship to their citizens in the form of slogans, posters, billboards, ads, and TV commercials."[73] At the heart of these moral pronouncements, he contends, are basic Confucian teachings such as respect for authority, honoring family and elders, being considerate, getting along with the group, and working hard. In the West, the task of passing on moral norms is left almost entirely to families and churches, Reid points out. In East Asian countries shaped by Confucianism, however, the entire

East Asian scholars struggle to find ways of applying Confucian ideals to modern economic goals.

community participates in inculcating values, and "you can see the results, in large ways and small, in the Confucian societies today,"[74] he says, citing crime, divorce, illegitimacy, and school dropout rates that are dramatically lower than those in the West.

In the Confucianized nations of East Asia, schools play an especially critical role in transmitting traditional moral values to young people. Although educational instruction has been thoroughly modernized in all these countries, most of their public schools still emphasize the teaching of Confucian ethics to each new generation. In Japan, writes Reid, "the unified national school system . . . was specifically designed to pass along traditional Confucian values, and has succeeded brilliantly at doing so."[75] In South Korea, the powerful National Confucian Association continually monitors primary and secondary schools to ensure that they pay adequate attention to Confucian ethics. In Taiwan, public school textbooks in social studies, literature, and other subjects include moral tales designed to illustrate core Confucian values such as loyalty, honesty, filial piety, and selfless compassion for others.

Reid and other modern commentators, who believe that Confucian values can help to shape better societies, maintain that one of Confucianism's greatest attributes is its insistence that the needs of the community always be placed above indi-

Confucianism in Modern Japan

In *Confucius Lives Next Door,* T. R. Reid notes that although the people of modern-day Japan still draw heavily on Confucian ethics in their ideas of morality and duty, they do not always recognize Confucius as the source of their attitudes regarding what constitutes virtuous behavior. "Schoolchildren learn about Confucius," writes Reid. "Years later, as adults, when they see a sign in the park saying 'Let's try not to do anything that will bother the other people,' they probably know that this is the kind of ethical rule the Confucian masters used to preach. But people don't go around quoting Confucius to each other. The moral teachings in signs and posters sometimes mention Confucius, but often they don't. The important thing is not the teacher but the teaching. The ancient lessons, the traditional rules of social behavior, are constantly reiterated."

vidual wants and ambitions. Confucius's strong emphasis on the virtues of ren (human-heartedness) and shu (treating others as you would want to be treated yourself) makes it clear that individualism had no place in his school of thought: The Master's ethical teachings were invariably other-centered. For Confucius, ren and all the moral traits that stemmed from it, such as loyalty, generosity, and reciprocity, were founded on a selfless concern for the welfare of others. People should endeavor to attain these virtues not merely for the sake of their own moral and spiritual development, but also for the benefit of the entire community, he stressed.

In accordance with Confucius's other-centered morality, in those East Asian countries shaped by the Confucian tradition, far more weight is placed on the family and community as a corporate entity, and far less on the rights of the individual than is generally true in Western nations. A strong communal feeling pervades the home, the classroom, the workplace, and society as a whole. Many East Asians believe that this emphasis on the rights and needs of the group over individual needs and rights is one of the most important lessons Confucianism can teach the West. Indeed, a number of East Asian political leaders and scholars have suggested that it is an exaggerated individualism, more than any other factor, that is responsible for the social problems that have troubled the United States and other Western nations in recent decades, including high crime rates and the breakdown of the nuclear family.

Yet even those—Easterner and Westerner alike—who have argued most strongly that Confucian virtues such as ren and generosity have relevance to contemporary society are quick to admit that not all of Confucius's teachings are appropriate or useful in today's world. In particular, traditional Confucian attitudes toward women have been criticized as being hopelessly outdated. In imperial China and other Confucianized countries such as Korea, women were taught to submit to their husbands and grown sons, and were generally considered less deserving of respect than men. "As a traditional doctrine that came into being in a patriarchal society, Confucianism held a low opinion of women,"[76] remarks the scholar Xinzhong Yao. According to Confucian beliefs, the truly virtuous woman had no educational, career, or political ambitions but instead was content to devote her entire life to serving her husband and caring for her home and children.

Today, few East Asian families or societies are as strongly patriarchal as the traditional Confucian family and society were. As one young Chinese woman recently told an American reporter attending the annual celebration in Qufu honoring the Master's birthday: "Confucius said that a wife should obey her husband . . . no matter what. That's an old-fashioned way of thinking. Who will accept that now?"[77] Indeed, today all women in the PRC must work outside their homes, in accordance with government policy. In South Korea, Japan, and other East Asian countries with a Confucian heritage, many married women also now work outside the home, in direct opposition to the Confucian ideal of the wife and mother who dedicated herself completely to her domestic responsibilities. In these countries, as in the West, few of even Confucianism's most ardent defenders have advocated turning back the clock to an earlier era, when many women were all but imprisoned within their homes. Yet, just because one element of Confucius's teachings needs to be discarded, they contend, that does not take away from the relevance of his other ideas for achieving the good society, such as compassion for others, propriety, or commitment to family and education.

The Political Relevance of Confucianism Today: Democracy Versus Dictatorship

Perhaps the most passionate current debate regarding the relevance of Confucianism to the modern world centers not on its social or economic usefulness, but rather on its political significance. The issue being discussed is whether Confucian teachings support democracy or authoritarianism.

Like virtually all systems of belief, Confucianism is open to widely differing interpretations. Over the last two thousand years, the sayings attributed to Confucius in the *Analects* have been understood in a variety of ways, "most of which reflect the biases of the interpreter,"[78] notes Linda Jakobson. Thus whether Confucian teachings are seen as promoting an authoritarian or a democratic political system depends first and foremost on who is doing the interpreting.

Coming down firmly on the side of the authoritarian interpretation of Confucianism is the autocratic government of the tiny yet highly populated island nation of Singapore. According to T. R. Reid, Singapore is "a world capital of the Confucian ethic, with Confucius's sayings taught in all schools and even set into the tile on the walls of the subway stations."[79] Given Singapore's strong attachment to its Confucian heritage, it seems natural that its rulers should seek support for their political attitudes and actions within Confucius's teachings. In the face of growing criticism of their autocratic practices, official spokesmen such as former prime minister Lee Kwan Yew have cited the ideas and values expressed by the Master time and time again in their efforts to defend their regime. To justify their authoritarian style of governance, they point to Confucius's teachings about the importance of subjects serving their leaders with absolute devotion and loyalty. To justify their strict approach to social control in which police equipped with binoculars spy on citizens from rooftops, Singapore's officials point to Confucius's deep concern with maintaining order and harmony within society.

The government of the PRC has joined Singapore's officials in linking traditional Confucian teachings to authoritarianism, insisting that Confucianism requires unquestioning submission to governmental authority. According to Francis Fukuyama, for the autocratic rulers of the PRC as well as for those of Singapore, "Asian" (i.e., Confucian) values conveniently offer "an apparently principled defense of their reluctance to broaden political participation" or support "human-rights practices."[80]

Yet, Confucianism has also been used in recent years to vindicate the expanding democracy movement in East Asia. Its champions argue that East Asian autocrats who claim to follow Confucian political philosophy have deliberately ignored crucial elements of the Master's teachings. Confucianism's true relevance for contemporary politics in Asia and throughout the world, they say, lies in its support for democratic ideals and practices. If Singapore's Lee Kuan Yew "can cite Confucian sources to support rule by benevolent authoritarianism," writes Fukuyama, backers of democracy in Taiwan, South Korea, and Japan can cite "other sources to prove the compatibility of Confucian tradition with . . . democratic institutions."[81]

In defense of their political views, East Asian proponents of democracy point out that Confucius taught that the chief purpose of government is to serve the best interests of the people. Although Confucius insisted that people owe their leaders loyalty, in Confucian ideology, they maintain, obligations between rulers and subjects run both ways—down as well as up. Rulers are obliged to treat their subjects with justice and benevolence and set a virtuous example for them to follow. The Master stood against oppression of any kind, the champions of democracy say, and extolled love and compassion for one's fellow human beings as the supreme virtue. They

The Role of Confucian Ritual in Modern East Asia

The pertinence and usefulness of traditional Confucian rituals in modern society have received little attention from academics, politicians, and social commentators, although some Confucian rites continue to be practiced in East Asia today. In many of the countries that adopted Confucianism outside of the PRC, the ancient ancestral rites that were so closely associated with the Master are still widely performed. The ancestral cult is especially important in South Korea, although today photographs of deceased relatives sometimes replace the customary wooden tablets on the family altar.

The most elaborate ancestral rituals being performed today in East Asia take place each year at the Chongmyo (Royal Ancestral Shrine) in South Korea. There the rites honoring the kings and queens of the Choson dynasty (1392–1910) are still carried out in accordance with age-old Confucian customs. On the first Sunday in May, incense, wine, and other offerings are made to the royal spirits in an intricate ceremony that features ancient dances and music. Once performed exclusively by men, typically students from Korea's National Confucian Academy, the dances and music are now performed by women as well.

At the Confucian shrine on the premises of the historic National Confucian Academy in Seoul, the traditional autumn and spring sacrifices are also performed in honor of Confucius and his leading Chinese and Korean disciples. On September 28, special ceremonies honoring Confucius's birthday are carried out in the academy's Confucian shrine as well as in the many ornate Confucian temples that dot the South Korean countryside. Ceremonies honoring Confucius are also held on that day in Confucian temples in a number of other East Asian countries, including Taiwan, where September 28 (Teachers' Day) was a national holiday until 1997.

Lee Kuan Yew, former prime minister of Singapore, justified his authoritarian rule by citing the teachings of Confucius.

also quote Mencius, the "Second Sage" of Confucianism, who wrote that people had a right to rebel against corrupt or tyrannical leaders. Among those who have argued the most forcefully that the seeds of democracy are contained in Confucianism is Kim Dae Jong. The leader of South Korea's democratic reform movement in the late 1980s and the nation's president since 1997, Kim Dae Jong is also a former university professor of Confucian thought.

The New Confucians

The relevance of Confucianism to today's world is an issue of central concern to the New Confucianism, the newest school of thought within the twenty-five-hundred-year-old philosophy.

Since the 1920s, a group of East Asian scholars known as the New Confucians have dedicated themselves to reforming Confucianism in hopes of adapting it to modern life. They are convinced that there is much in the tradition worth saving. Above all, they want to revive central Confucian values such as ren, shu, and loyalty and make them relevant to contemporary circumstances. Most New Confucians do not reject Western learning or culture, but contend that the East and West have much to learn from one another. The lesson many believe Westerners most urgently need to glean from the Confucian tradition is the paramount importance of human values and responsibilities over the pursuit of money and material objects.

The New Confucians argue that the Confucian ideals of individual moral greatness through self-cultivation and education and of a harmonious society are as relevant to the modern age as they were when Confucius walked the earth some twenty-five hundred years ago. They realize that Confucianism will probably never again hold the dominant place in East Asian political ideology or administration that it once did. They accept that most of the religious rites once associated with Confucianism, from grand state ceremonies such as the Cult of Heaven to the sacrifices made to Confucius himself, are fading away or have already disappeared for good. Yet, they believe that the spirit of Confucianism will live on and that its fundamental moral teachings are as pertinent as they ever were to personal and social life.

South Korean president Kim Dae Jong believes that Confucian principles of fairness and compassion support democratic ideals and practices.

H. G. Creel, one of Confucius's most respected Western interpreters, writes that those searching for the secret of the Master's abiding appeal will likely find it "in his insistence upon the supremacy of human values. Wisdom, he said, is to know men; virtue is to love men." Perhaps even more significant in explaining Confucius's enduring importance, Creel continues, was that unlike most philosophers, Confucius trusted people to think for themselves. Indeed, he notes, "Confucius was not only willing that people should think for themselves; he insisted upon it. He was willing to help them and to teach them *how* to think, but the answers they must find for themselves."[82] Perhaps the twenty-first century will bring a new appreciation in the West as well as in the East for how Confucius's ancient teachings can guide people in finding answers to the pressing moral and social problems they must confront in a rapidly changing world.

Appendix

The Pinyin System

Chinese writing does not use alphabetic characters. Instead, it uses pictographs to symbolize simplified pictures of an object and ideographs to symbolize an idea such as compassion or wisdom. Over the years, different phonetic systems were developed to "romanize" the sounds of spoken Chinese into the letters used in the Roman alphabet. This book uses the pinyin system of romanization, which was formally adopted by the Chinese government in 1979. Before 1979, the most popular system for translating Chinese words into English was the Wade-Giles system. Names familiar to Western readers in older forms such as Wade-Giles appear in those forms in this book—for example, Confucius, Mencius, and Chiang Kai-shek.

Spelling Guide

Since some texts still use the Wade-Giles system of romanizing Chinese words, the following chart gives the pinyin and Wade-Giles forms of many of the names and terms found in this book.

PINYIN	WADE-GILES
Daoism (dao)	Taoism (tao)
Dong Zhongshu	Tung Chung-shu
Junzi	Chun-tzu
Kong Fuzi	Kung Fu-tzu (Confucius)
Laozi	Lao Tzu
Mao Zedong	Mao Tse-tung
Mengzi	Meng Tzu (Mencius)
Qin	Ch'in
Qing	Ch'ing
Ren	Jen
Xunzi	Hsun Tzu
Zhou	Chou
Zhu Xi	Chu Hsi

Notes

Chapter One: Confucius: His Life and Times: 551 B.C.–479 B.C.

1. *The Analects of Confucius*. Trans. David Hinton, Washington, DC: Counterpoint, 1998, 9:6, p. 92.
2. *Analects*, 2:4, p. 11.
3. *Analects*, 7:20, p. 72.
4. Quoted in Valerie Hansen, *The Open Empire: A History of China to 1600*. New York: W. W. Norton, 2000, p. 45.
5. *Analects*, 5:27, p. 51.
6. *Analects*, 1:1, p. 3.
7. *Analects*, 7:8, p. 68.
8. *Analects*, 4:11, 4:16, pp. 35, 36.
9. H. G. Creel, *Chinese Thought: From Confucius to Mao Tse-Tung*. Chicago: University of Chicago Press, 1953, p. 42.
10. *Analects*, 7:7, p. 68.
11. *Analects*, 8:17, p. 85.
12. *Analects*, 7:19, p. 71.
13. *Analects*, 6:2, p. 55.
14. *Analects*, 6:10, p. 58.
15. *Analects*, 13:10, p. 142.
16. D. Howard Smith, *Confucius*. New York: Charles Scribner's Sons, 1973, p. 43.
17. *Analects*, 17:7, p. 197.
18. *Analects*, 11:9, p. 115.
19. *Analects*, 7:35, p. 76.

Chapter Two: Confucianism Emerges: The Fifth Through the Third Centuries B.C.

20. *Analects*, 7:1, p. 67.
21. *Analects*, 4:5, p. 33.
22. *Analects*, 12:22, p. 134.
23. Luke 6:31, Authorized (King James) Version and *Analects*, 12:2, p. 127.
24. *Analects*, 6:29, p. 62.
25. *Analects*, 1:2, p. 3.
26. *Analects*, 2:5, p. 12.
27. *Analects*, 10:3, p. 103.
28. *Analects*, 10:7, p. 106.
29. *Analects*, 10:19, p. 109.
30. *Analects*, 3:26, p. 28.
31. *Analects*, 12:19, p. 133.
32. *Analects*, 2:3, p. 11.
33. *Analects*, 2:14, p. 14.
34. *Analects*, 16:1, p. 185.
35. *Analects*, 14:35, p. 163.
36. *Analects*, 3:13, p. 24.
37. *Analects*, 7:23, p. 72.
38. *Analects*, 11:12, p. 116.
39. Smith, *Confucius*, p. 61.
40. *Analects*, 2:17, p. 15.
41. Quoted in Ch'u Chai and Winberg Chai, *Confucianism*. Hauppauge, NY: Barron's Educational Series, 1973, pp. 51–52.
42. Quoted in Smith, *Confucius*, pp. 102–103.

Chapter Three: The Changing Fortunes of Confucianism in China: The Qin Through the Tang Dynasties: 221 B.C.–A.D. 960

43. Christian Jochim, *Chinese Religions: A Cultural Perspective*. Englewood Cliffs, NJ: Prentice Hall, 1986, p. 62.
44. Chai and Chai, *Confucianism,* p. 101.
45. Smith, *Confucius,* p. 111.
46. Smith, *Confucius,* p. 130.
47. Creel, *Chinese Thought,* p. 114.
48. Quoted in John K. Shryock, *The Origin and Development of the State Cult of Confucius: An Introductory Study*. New York: Paragon Book Reprint, 1966, pp. 169–70.
49. Julia Ching, *Chinese Religions.* Maryknoll, NY: Orbis Books, 1993, p. 62.

Chapter Four: The Apex of Confucianism: Confucianism in China and East Asia from the Tenth to the Twentieth Centuries

50. Xinzhong Yao, *An Introduction to Confucianism.* Cambridge, UK: Cambridge University Press, 2000, p. 106.
51. Smith, *Confucius,* p. 159.
52. Quoted in Yao, *An Introduction to Confucianism,* p. 206.
53. Ching, *Chinese Religions,* p. 60.
54. C. C. Chai and W. Chai, eds., *Li Chi, Book of Rites.* 2 vols. Trans. James Legge. New York: University Books, 1967, Vol. 2, pp. 429–30.
55. *Li Chi, Book of Rites,* chap. 12, Vol. 1, pp. 450–51.
56. John H. Berthrong and Evelyn Nagai Berthrong, *Confucianism: A Short Introduction*. Oxford, UK: One World, 2000, p. 5.
57. Ching, *Chinese Religions,* p. 165.
58. Quoted in Ryusaku Tsunoda, Wm. Theodore de Bary, and Donald Keene, eds., *Sources of Japanese Tradition.* 2 vols. New York: Columbia University Press, 1960, Vol. 1, p. 391.

Chapter Five: From Vilification to Rehabilitation: Confucianism in Twentieth-Century China

59. de Bary, *Sources of Chinese Tradition,* p. 727.
60. Berthrong and Berthrong, *Confucianism,* p. 179.
61. Ching, *Chinese Religions,* p. 166.
62. Quoted in Yao, *An Introduction to Confucianism,* p. 252.
63. Quoted in Willem Van Kemenade, *China, Hong Kong, Taiwan, Inc.* New York: Alfred A. Knopf, 1997, p. 373.
64. Julian F. Pas, ed., *The Turning of the Tide: Religion in China Today*. New York: Oxford University Press, 1989, p. 13.
65. Quoted in Mabel Lee and A. D. Syrokomla-Stefanowska, eds., *Modernization of the Chinese Past.* Sydney, Australia: Wild Peony, 1993, p. 20.

66. J. R. Levenson, *Confucianism and Its Modern Fate.* Vol. 3. Berkeley: University of California Press, 1964, p. 62.
67. Pas, *The Turning of the Tide,* p. 14.

Chapter Six: The Relevance of Confucianism Today

68. Van Kemenade, *China,* p. 368.
69. Van Kemenade, *China,* p. 371.
70. Quoted in Van Kemenade, *China,* p. 372.
71. Quoted in Linda Jakobson, *A Million Truths: A Decade in China.* New York: M. Evans, 1998, p. 205.
72. Francis Fukuyama, "Asian Values and the Asian Crisis," *Commentary,* February 1998, p. 11.
73. T. R. Reid, *Confucius Lives Next Door: What Living in the East Teaches Us about Living in the West.* New York: Random House, 1999, pp. 166–67.
74. Reid, *Confucius Lives Next Door,* p. 174.
75. Reid, *Confucius Lives Next Door,* p. 117.
76. Yao, *An Introduction to Confucianism,* p. 183.
77. Quoted in Seth Faison, "Not Equal to Confucius, but Friends to His Memory," *New York Times,* October 10, 1997, p. 4.
78. Jakobson, *A Million Truths,* p. 204.
79. Reid, *Confucius Lives Next Door,* p. 260.
80. Fukuyama, "Asian Values," p. 12.
81. Fukuyama, "Asian Values," p. 13.
82. Creel, *Chinese Thought,* p. 44.

Glossary

Analects (Lunyu): A record of the sayings and opinions of Confucius that his followers compiled after his death.

Ancestor worship: The performance of rituals honoring the ancestral spirits of families. Confucius considered it an important part of filial piety, or devotion toward parents.

Buddhism: Founded by Gautama Buddha in India in the 500s B.C., Buddhism first arrived in China during the Han dynasty. It teaches that life is suffering and the only way to escape its endless cycles of birth, aging, sickness, and death is to renounce all earthly desires and follow the Eightfold Path of right behavior and belief.

Daoism: Founded by the legendary sixth-century B.C. sage Laozi, Daoism began as a philosophy but eventually evolved into a popular religion. It emphasizes living in harmony with the Dao, the source and unity of all life.

Dynasty: A hereditary ruling house.

Feudalism: A political, social, and economic system based on bargains made between a sovereign and his vassals or noble subjects.

Filial piety (xiao): One of the central Confucian virtues, it entails respect, devotion, and obedience toward parents.

Five Classics *(Wujing)*: The *Book of Poetry, Book of Rites, Book of History, Book of Changes,* and *Spring and Autumn Annals.* They form the heart of the Confucian canon along with the Four Books and were studied by candidates for Chinese civil service examinations from the Han dynasty until the twentieth century.

Five Elements: In traditional Chinese thought, the five elements that compose all things: earth, water, fire, metal, and wood. They are closely linked with the concepts of yin/yang.

Five Relationships: In Confucianism, the five fundamental relationships underlying an orderly and harmonious society: father-son, husband-wife, older brother–younger brother, ruler-subject, friend-friend.

Four Books: The four classic Confucian texts selected by the great Neo-Confucian philosopher Zhu Xi to be the core of Confucian education: the *Analects, Book of Mencius, Great Learning,* and *Doctrine of the Mean.* They were the central focus of the civil service examination system in China from the early 1300s until the early 1900s.

Heaven: The supreme deity in traditional Chinese religion.

Junzi: The Confucian ideal of the "noble-minded one": a gentleman distinguished not for his noble birth but rather for his superior virtue and wisdom.

Legalism: A school of thought adopted by China's first emperor, Shi Huangdi. It emphasized the importance of the state and the need to control people with strong laws.

Li: (1) The traditional Chinese code of rituals and etiquette. (2) In Neo-Confucianism, another name for principle, the nonphysical essence inherent within all that exists.

Mandate of Heaven: The traditional Chinese belief that Heaven bestowed kings with the authority or mandate to rule and could remove it if the rulers became corrupt.

Mencius (Mengzi) (ca. 372–289 B.C.): Known as the Second Sage, Mencius was an influential early interpreter of Confucius's teachings. He asserted that people are naturally good.

Neo-Confucianism: A reinterpretation of Confucianism dominant from the Song dynasty to the twentieth century in China and much of East Asia, it borrowed some concepts from Buddhism and Daoism.

Rectification of Names: The Confucian concept that people must strive to fulfill the duties associated with each position they occupy or role they must perform.

Ren: The supreme virtue according to Confucius. It is usually translated as "humanity" or "human-heartedness" and basically means compassion for other people.

Shi: In ancient China, people who could claim aristocratic forebears but possessed little wealth or land of their own. They usually held military or low-level government positions.

Shu: A virtue closely linked to the supreme Confucian virtue of ren, it means reciprocity—"never impose on others what you would not choose for yourself" (*Analects,* 12:2).

Six Arts: The traditional curriculum for young Chinese gentlemen, it included archery, chariot driving, arithmetic, music, calligraphy (the art of beautiful handwriting), and li (etiquette and ritual).

Xunzi (ca. 310–230 B.C.): The third important shaper of Confucianism after Confucius and Mencius, he believed that human nature was fundamentally evil.

Yin/Yang: The two complementary principles in nature according to traditional Chinese thought. Yin is the passive, female aspect and yang the active, male one.

Zhu Xi (1130–1200): The most influential of the Neo-Confucian philosophers, he incorporated ideas from Buddhism and Daoism into Confucianism and chose the Four Books as the basis for Confucian learning.

For Further Reading

Chih Chung Tsai, *Words to Live By: Confucius Speaks.* New York: Doubleday, 1996. Created by one of East Asia's most popular cartoonists, this illustrated collection of the sayings of Confucius brings the sage and his teachings to life.

"Confucius and Confucianism," *Calliope,* October 1999. The entire issue is devoted to Confucius and the development of Confucianism.

Arthur Cotterell, *Eyewitness Books: Ancient China.* New York: Alfred A. Knopf, 1994. This richly illustrated book includes information on day-to-day life as well as political, military, and cultural developments.

Eleanor J. Hall, *Ancient Chinese Dynasties.* San Diego: Lucent Books, 2000. A well-researched account of ancient Chinese history up to the Tang dynasty.

"The Han Dynasty of China," *Calliope,* October 1998. The entire issue is devoted to the Han dynasty, with special attention to the influence of Confucianism during the period.

Thomas Hoobler and Dorothy Hoobler, *Confucianism.* New York: Facts On File, 1993. A detailed account of the development and influence of Confucianism over the centuries.

Betty Kelen, *Confucius in Life and Legend.* New York: Thomas Nelson, 1971. A well-written biography for young people.

Michael G. Kort, *China Under Communism.* Brookfield, CT: Millbrook Press, 1994. This book includes a discussion of the plight of Con-fucianism and religion in general under Communist rule.

Robert E. Murowchick, ed., *China: Ancient Culture, Modern Land.* Norman: University of Oklahoma Press, 1994. A carefully researched and beautifully illustrated book for older students and adults.

Josh Wilker, *Confucius: Philosopher and Teacher.* Danbury, CT: Franklin Watts, 1999. A well-researched biography for young people.

Works Consulted

Books

The Analects of Confucius. Trans. David Hinton. Washington, DC: Counterpoint, 1998. This recent translation of the collected sayings of Confucius includes a useful introductory essay.

John H. Berthrong and Evelyn Nagai Berthrong, *Confucianism: A Short Introduction*. Oxford, UK: One World, 2000. An informative guide to the history, teachings, and present state of Confucianism.

Caroline Blunden and Mark Elvin, *Cultural Atlas of China*. New York: Facts On File, 1998. A carefully researched cultural history of China.

Richard Bowring and Peter Kornicki, eds., *The Cambridge Encyclopedia of Japan*. Cambridge, UK: Cambridge University Press, 1993. This carefully researched and richly illustrated volume contains a useful section on the history and current status of Confucianism in Japan.

Ch'u Chai and Winberg Chai, *Confucianism*. Hauppauge, NY: Barron's Educational Series, 1973. Clearly explains the fundamental teachings of Confucianism.

C. C. Chai and W. Chai, eds. *Li Chi, Book of Rites*. 2 vols. Trans. James Legge. New York: University Books, 1967. An English translation of one of the most influential books in the Confucian canon.

Julia Ching, *Chinese Religions*. Maryknoll, NY: Orbis Books, 1993. Includes sections on the history of China's indigenous religious traditions, including Confucianism, and on the influence of foreign religions in China over the centuries.

H. G. Creel, *Chinese Thought: From Confucius to Mao Tse-Tung*. Chicago: University of Chicago Press, 1953. A clear account of the main trends in Chinese philosophy by one of the most respected scholars of Chinese thought and history.

H. G. Creel, *Confucius: The Man and the Myth*. New York: John Day, 1949. A classic study of Confucius's life and teachings by a leading scholar.

Wm. Theodore de Bary, *Sources of Chinese Tradition*. New York: Columbia University Press, 1960. Includes excerpts from important sources in Chinese history and culture including such Confucian classics as the *Book of History*, *Analects*, and *Book of Mencius*.

Fung Yu-Lan with Derk Bodde, *A Short History of Chinese Philosophy*. New

York: Macmillan, 1948. This overview of Chinese philosophy from ancient times through the first half of the twentieth century includes helpful chapters on Confucianism and Neo-Confucianism.

Valerie Hansen, *The Open Empire: A History of China to 1600*. New York: W. W. Norton, 2000. Using the most recent archaeological evidence, Hansen examines everyday life as well as major political and economic trends in Chinese history to 1600.

Stephen Haw, *China: A Cultural History*. London: B. T. Batsford, 1990. A useful reference on Chinese culture from ancient times to the present.

Linda Jakobson, *A Million Truths: A Decade in China*. New York: M. Evans, 1998. Jakobson, who has lived and worked in China, discusses the great changes that occurred in Chinese society and attitudes during the last two decades of the twentieth century.

Christian Jochim, *Chinese Religions: A Cultural Perspective*. Englewood Cliffs, NJ: Prentice Hall, 1986. Discusses the ideology, practices, and history of Confucianism as well as of China's other major religions.

Mabel Lee and A. D. Syrokomla-Stefanowska, eds., *Modernization of the Chinese Past*. Sydney, Australia: Wild Peony, 1993. Includes essays on Confucianism and its relationship to recent Asian political and economic developments.

J. R. Levenson, *Confucianism and Its Modern Fate*. Vol. 3. Berkeley: University of California Press, 1964. A scholarly discussion of Confucianism's place in the modern world.

C. Scott Littleton, ed., *Eastern Wisdom: An Illustrated Guide to the Religions and Philosophies of the East*. New York: Henry Holt, 1996. A clearly written and attractively illustrated volume.

Donald Lopez Jr., ed., *Religions of China in Practice*. Princeton, NJ: Princeton University Press, 1996. Describes how China's major religions—Confucianism, Daoism, and Buddhism—interact with each other.

Julian F. Pas, ed., *The Turning of the Tide: Religion in China Today*. New York: Oxford University Press, 1989. Includes an interesting chapter on the annual ceremonies in Qufu in honor of Confucius's birthday.

T. R. Reid, *Confucius Lives Next Door: What Living in the East Teaches Us about Living in the West*. New York: Random House, 1999. The author, a journalist who lived and worked in East Asia for many years, discusses the role that Confucian values played in creating the East Asian "social miracle"—low crime rates, stable families, and outstanding educational systems.

John K. Shryock, *The Origin and Development of the State Cult of Confucius: An Introductory Study.* New York: Paragon Book Reprint, 1966. Discusses Confucianism's connection with China's traditional state religion from the Han through the Qing dynasties.

D. Howard Smith, *Confucius.* New York: Charles Scribner's Sons, 1973. A well-written account of the life of Confucius and the development of Confucianism during the centuries following his death.

Paul Strathern, *Confucius in Ninety Minutes.* Chicago: Ivan R. Dee, 1999. A concise account of Confucius's life and teachings.

Ryusaku Tsunoda, Wm. Theodore de Bary, and Donald Keene, eds., *Sources of Japanese Tradition.* 2 vols. New York: Columbia University Press, 1958. Includes excerpts from important Japanese works of philosophy, including the writings of leading Confucians.

Willem Van Kemenade, *China, Hong Kong, Taiwan, Inc.* New York: Alfred A. Knopf, 1997. Includes a thoughtful discussion of the current role as well as the future of Confucianism in China and East Asia.

Xinzhong Yao, *An Introduction to Confucianism.* Cambridge, UK: Cam-bridge University Press, 2000. This study of Confucianism's main doctrines, schools, and rituals provides a detailed account of how Confucianism operated in the past and its significance for the present.

Periodicals

"Asian Values Revisited: What Would Confucius Say Now?" *Economist*, July 25, 1998. Discusses the recent scholarly debate over whether Confucian values have harmed or helped East Asia's economy.

Robert Bruce, "The Return to Confucius?" *History Today*, January 1998. Discusses the changing attitude of the Chinese government toward Confucianism.

Seth Faison, "Not Equal to Confucius, but Friends to His Memory," *New York Times*, October 10, 1997. An account of the recent birthday celebrations held in honor of Confucius in his hometown of Qufu, China.

Francis Fukuyama, "Asian Values and the Asian Crisis," *Commentary*, February 1998. Discusses Confucian values and their relation to East Asia's economy and society.

Index

Ai, duke of, 92
Analects
- basis of Confucianism and, 28
- on Confucius's life, 11, 21, 23, 27, 28
- Confucius's reverence of Heaven in, 37
- on filial piety, 31
- Latin version of, 77
- on li, 33
- as one of the Four Books, 65, 66
- rediscovery after the Qin era, 48
- selections from, 30
- varied interpretations of, 109
- virtue of human-heartedness in, 29
- Voltaire on, 77

ancestor cults/worship
- in China, 17–18
- in Communist China, 95–99
- Confucianism and, 71
- in modern East Asia, 110

Association for Research on Confucius, 93
authoritarianism, 109–10

Ban Zhao, 53
Bary, Wm. Theodore de, 85
Berthrong, Evelyn, 73, 87
Berthrong, John 73, 87
Board of Rites, 68
Book of Changes, 15–16, 26, 27, 50
Book of Documents. See Book of History
Book of History
- in Confucian education, 50
- Confucius's study of, 15, 16
- question of Confucius's editing of, 26, 27
- survival during Qin era, 48
- taught by Confucius in his school, 21

Book of Mencius, 41, 65, 66
Book of Odes. See Book of Poetry
Book of Poetry
- in Confucian education, 50
- Confucius's study of, 16–17
- poem on ancestors, 18
- question of Confucius's editing of, 26, 27
- taught by Confucius in his school, 21

Book of Rites
- in Confucian education, 50
- family rituals and, 70–71
- on filial piety, 72–73
- in Korea, 75
- on marriage rites, 71–72
- printing of, 70–71
- question of Confucius's editing of, 26
- sacrifice to Heaven and, 68
- as source of *Doctrine of the Mean* and *Great Learning*, 65, 66
- on widows, 80

books
- bookmaking in Confucius's time, 15
- burning in the Qin era, 47

Boxers, 84
Buddhism
- in Korea, 73
- lack of practical political philosophy in, 58
- Neo-Confucianism and, 63–64, 65
- during the Period of Disunity, 46, 52, 54–56
- during the Tang dynasty, 56–57, 63
- in Vietnam, 79
- Wang Yangming and, 64
- Wheel of Life, 57

Chiang Kai-shek, 87–89
China
- ancestor worship, 17–18, 71, 95–99
- Chinese Republic, 86–89
- civil service examination system, 50, 56, 57, 66–68, 86
- cult of Confucius, 58–61, 69–70
- dynasties, 12
- education in Confucius's time, 13–15
- era of feudalism and feudal warfare, 19–20, 39–40, 45
- family rituals, 70–73
- Han dynasty, 8, 26, 48–52, 60, 73
- "Hundred Schools of Thought" era, 40
- invasions by Japan, 83, 89
- Kang Youwei's reforms, 85–86
- mandate of Heaven concept, 12
- Ming dynasty, 73
- Neo-Confucianism and, 65–66
- Period of Disunity, 52, 54–56
- Qin dynasty, 45, 46–48
- Qing dynasty, 12, 65, 82–85
- relations with Western powers, 82–85
- Song dynasty, 63, 70–71
- state religious rites, 68–69
- Tang era, 56–61, 63
- Vietnam and, 78
- *see also* People's Republic of China

Chinese Communist Party, 89
- *see also* People's Republic of China

Chinese Republic, 86–89
Ching, Julia, 60, 70, 75, 87
Chongmyo Shrine, 110
Choson dynasty (Korea), 73, 96
civil service examination system
- abandoned during the Period of Disunity, 56
- abolition of, 86
- development of, 50
- dominated by Neo-Confucianism, 66–68
- revival of, 57

coming-of-age, 71
Communism, 89
- *see also* People's Republic of China

community, East Asian Confucianism and, 107–108
Confucian education
- civil service examination system, 50, 56, 57, 66–68, 86
- Confucius's beliefs and practices, 21–24
- in East Asia, 107
- Five Classics and, 49–50
- in Korea, 73–74
- state-sponsored system in the Han era, 49–50
- women and, 53
- *see also* education

Confucianism

authoritarian governments and, 109–10
basis of, 28–29
characteristics of philosophy and religion in, 9–10
in the Chinese Republic, 87–89
civil service examination system, 50, 56, 57, 66–68, 86
in Communist China
influence on everyday life, 94–97
under Mao, 89–91
rehabilitation following Mao, 91–93
relevance to current challenges, 98–102
used to support authoritarian rule, 109–10
continuing importance of, 8–9, 113
cult of Confucius, 58–61, 69–70
democracy movements and, 109, 110–11
in East Asia, 8–9, 73, 96
democracy movement and, 110–11
economic miracle and, 102–105
New Confucianism, 112–13
social miracle and, 105–108
economy and, 102–105
family rituals, 70–73
Five Classics, 26, 49–50, 57, 66
during the Han dynasty, 58
Ban Zhou, 53
becomes state doctrine, 8, 49–50
incorporation of yin/yang and Five Elements philosophies, 50–52
influence within the government, 48–49
importance of education in, 36, 42, 43
in Japan, 74, 75–78, 96, 106
Kang Youwei's reforms, 85–86
in Korea, 73–75, 96
li in, 33–35
May Fourth movement, 87
Mencius and, 39, 40–42, 43–44
moral philosophy of, 29–31
New Life movement, 88–89
numbers of modern Confucians, 9
during the Period of Disunity, 52, 54–56
persecution under the Qin dynasty, 46–48
political philosophy of, 34–37
during the Qing dynasty, 82, 84–85
religious thought and, 9, 37–39, 54, 92–93
social philosophy of, 31–33
during the Tang dynasty, 56–61, 63
in Vietnam, 63, 78–80, 96
in the Western world, 77
women and, 53, 108
Xunzi and, 42–44
Confucian scholar-officials
civil service examination system and, 50, 56, 57, 66–68, 86
Confucian political philosophy, 35–37
cult of Confucius and, 58–59
decline during the Period of Disunity, 56
domination of state religious rites, 68–69
influence during the Han dynasty, 48–49, 50
in Korea, 73
in the Tang era, 57, 58–59
views of business activities, 105
Confucian schools
in East Asia, 107
founded by Confucius, 21–24
in Korea, 73–74
national university of the Han dynasty, 49–50
Confucian social philosophy
East Asian social miracle and, 105–108
family order, 31–32
filial piety, 31
Five Relationships, 32
rectification of names, 32–33
Confucian temples
attacked during the Cultural Revolution, 90–91
ceremonies in honor of Confucius, 69–70, 93
Emperor Taizong's order to build, 58–59
in Korea, 73–74
in modern East Asia, 10, 110
at Qufu, 70, 90–91, 92, 93
Confucian virtues
filial piety, 31
moral education and, 42
in Neo-Confucianism, 65
ren, 29, 30, 31
shu, 30–31
Xunzi and, 43
Confucius
basis of Confucianism and, 8, 28–29
birth of, 12
career in government, 15, 24–25
cult of, 58–61, 69–70
death of, 27
family background, 12–13
given name, 12
Jiang Zemin on, 94
junzi concept and, 36–37
later years of, 25–27
legends of, 60
li and, 33–34
mandate of Heaven concept and, 35
Mao Zedong's hatred of, 89–90
marriage of, 15
moral philosophy of, 29–31
mourning for mother's death, 17–18
notions of filial piety and family order, 31–32
political philosophy, 34–37
religious thought and, 10, 37–39
self-proclaimed mission of, 28
social philosophy of, 31–33
as student and learner, 11, 13–17, 18–19, 24, 27
as teacher and scholar, 19–24
on understanding, 39
Confucius: The Man and the Myth (Creel), 77
Confucius Lives Next Door (Reid), 103, 106
corporal punishment, 35
Creel, H. G., 23, 58, 77, 113
Cultural Revolution, 90–91

dao, 38, 52, 55
Dao De Jing, 55
Daoism
lack of practical political philosophy in, 58

Neo-Confucianism and, 63–64, 65
during the Period of Disunity, 46, 52, 54, 55–56
during the Tang dynasty, 56–57, 63
death
Confucius on, 39
mourning rituals, 17–18, 75
democracy movements, 109, 110–11
divination, 16
Doctrine of the Mean, 65, 66
Dong Zhongshu, 49, 51
dynasties, 12

East Asia
Confucianism and the economic miracle, 102–105
Confucianism and the social miracle, 105–108
Confucianism spreads to, 73
Confucian temples, 10, 110
democracy movement, 110–11
modern influence of Confucianism, 8–9, 96
New Confucianism, 112–13
women in, 108
economy, 102–105
education
in China, 13–15
Confucius's beliefs and practices, 21–24
importance in Confucianism, 36, 42, 43
moral, 42
women and, 53
See also Confucian education
Eightfold Path, 57
"eight steps," 66
Ekken, Kaibara. *See* Kaibara Ekken
elements. *See* Five Elements theory
emperors
Japanese, 77
state religious rites and, 68
See also rulers
Essentials of the New Life Movement (Chiang Kai-shek), 88
ethics
in Confucian thought, 29–31
Japanese samurai and, 74, 77–78
etiquette, 14–15. *see also* li

evil, 42, 43

family
Confucian ideal of order in, 31–32
filial piety, 31
policies in Communist China, 95, 96
feasts, in ancestor worship, 18
Feng Sheng, 48
feudalism, 19–20, 39–40
filial piety
Book of Rites on, 72–73
in Communist China, 94–95
in Confucian thought, 31
in Korean Confucianism, 75
Mencius on, 44
Vietnamese Confucianism and, 80
Five Classics, 26, 49–50, 57, 66
Five Elements theory, 51–52
Five Relationships, 32, 77
Four Books, 65, 66
Fukuyama, Francis, 105, 109, 111

Gautama Buddha, 57
ghosts, 39
good, 40–42
government official(s)
Confucian political philosophy and, 35–37
Confucius's career as, 15, 24–25
junzi ideal, 36–37
See also Confucian scholar-officials; rulers
Great Britain, 82–83
Great Learning, 65, 66
"Great Sacrifices," 68
Guangxu (emperor), 85
Guomindang, 86–87, 89

Han dynasty
Ban Zhao, 53
Book of Rites and, 26
Confucian influence in government, 48–49
Confucianism becomes state doctrine, 8, 49–50
cult of Confucius in, 58
evolution of Confucian thought during, 50–52
legends of Confucius, 60

spread of Confucianism to Korea, 73
Hansen, Valerie, 18, 53
Hayashi Razan, 74
Heaven (supreme god)
Confucius's reverence for, 37–38
mandate of, 12, 35
moral behavior and, 38
state religious rites and, 68
Hinton, David, 30
Hong Kong, 83
see also East Asia
Huan T'ui, 38
human-heartedness, 29, 65
see also ren
human nature
Mencius's theory of, 40–42, 43
Xunzi's philosophy of, 43
"Hundred Schools of Thought" era, 40

Ieyasu, 74, 76, 77
individualism, 107, 108

Jakobson, Linda, 102, 109
Japan
Confucian ethics and samurai, 74
introduction and early influence of Confucianism, 62, 75–78
invasion
China, 83, 89
Korea, 83
modern influence of Confucianism, 96, 106, 107, 108
women in, 108
see also East Asia
Jesuits, 77
Jiang Zemin, 94
Jochim, Christian, 48, 49
junzi, 36–37
Kaibara Ekken, 78
Kang Youwei, 85–86
Kemenade, Willem Van, 99–100
Kim Dai Jong, 111
"Kong Fuzi." *See* Confucius
Kong Qiu. *See* Confucius
Korea
introduction and influence of Confucianism, 62, 73–75
invasion by Japan, 83

modern influence of Confucianism, 96
see also South Korea

Laozi, 52, 55
Lee Kuan Yew, 109, 111
Legalism, 46, 47
legends, of Confucius, 60
Lessons for Women (Ban Zhao), 53
Levenson, J. R., 94
li
classic rules of, 14–15
in Confucianism, 33–35
Han rulers and, 48–49
in Neo-Confucianism, 64, 65
in the Period of Disunity, 56
political leaders and, 34–35
see also rituals, family
libraries, 15
Li Lanqing, 100, 101
Lu (state), 12, 15, 20, 25, 26
Lu, duke of, 25
Lunyu. See Analects
lute. *See* scholar's lute

Manchus, 82
Mandarins, 67
Mao Zedong, 89–90, 91, 94
marriage, 71–72, 95
Master Kong. *See* Confucius
May Fourth movement, 87
Mencius
importance to Confucianism, 28, 39, 46
political philosophy of, 41
quoted by modern democracy movements, 111
theory of human nature, 40–42, 43
Mengzi. *See* Mencius
Ming dynasty, 65, 73
music, 14, 70
myths, of Confucius, 60

National Confucian Academy (South Korea), 110
National Confucian Association (South Korea), 107
Nationalist Party. *See* Guomindang
Neo-Confucianism
in Japan, 76–78
in Korea, 74
overview of, 63–66
New Confucianism, 112–13
New Life movement, 88–89
Nguyen family, 96
Nirvana, 54, 57
noblesse oblige, 29
"Noble Truth," 57

"obediences," 53
Open Empire, The (Hansen), 18, 53
opium trade, 82–83

Pas, Julian, 91, 92, 95
patriarchy, 31–32
Peking, 69, 87
People's Republic of China
attacks on Confucianism, 89–91
Confucianism and modernization, 91–93
Confucianism in support of authoritarianism, 109–10
influence of Confucianism on everyday life, 94–97
relevance of Confucianism to current challenges, 98–102
rise of, 89
Tiananmen Square demonstration, 99
women in, 108
Period of Disunity, 46, 52, 54–56
philosophy
moral
Confucian, 29–31
Mencius's theory of human nature, 40–42, 43
moral path of Heaven, 38
Xunzi's theory of human nature, 43
political
Buddhist and Daoist deficiencies in, 58
of Confucius, 34–37
of Mencius, 41
of Xunzi, 43
prayers, 59
principle, in Neo-Confucianism, 64, 65
punishment, 35

qi, 64–65
qin, 14
Qin dynasty, 45, 46–48
Qing dynasty, 12, 65, 82–85
Qufu, 23, 27, 58
see also Temple of Confucius (Qufu)

Razan. *See* Hayashi Razan
rebellion, 41, 111
reciprocity. *See* shu
Red Guards, 90
Reid, T. R., 103, 106, 109
religion, 68–69
ren
in Confucian thought, 29, 30, 31, 107
Mencius on, 44
in Neo-Confucianism, 65
Republic of China, 89
Ricci, Matteo, 77
rituals
classic rules of li, 14–15
coming-of-age, 71
Confucian
ceremonies in honor of Confucius, 58–60, 69–70, 93
in modern East Asia, 110
family
ancestor worship, 17–18, 71, 95–99
Book of Rites and, 70–71
coming-of-age, 71
in Communist China, 95–96
filial piety, 72–73
Korean Confucianism and, 74–75
marriage, 71–72
Zhu Xi's manual on, 71
of mourning, 17–18, 75
state religious rites, 68–69
Royal Ancestral Shrine (South Korea), 110
Rozman, Gilbert, 103
rulers
in Confucian political philosophy, 34–37
in Mencius's political philosophy, 41
sage kings, 16, 22
in Xunzi's political philosophy, 43

sacrifices
in the cult of Confucius, 69, 70
in state religious rites, 68–69

sage kings, 16, 22
samurai, 74, 76, 77–78
scholar's lute, 14
School of Mind, 64
School of Principle, 63, 64
    see also Neo-Confucianism
schools. *See* Confucian schools
secret societies, 84
Shangdong (province), 93
Shang dynasty, 12
shi class, 12–13
Shi Huangdi (emperor), 46, 47
Shijing. See Book of Poetry
Shinto, 77
shogun, 76
shu, 30–31, 107
Shujing. See Book of History
Singapore, 106, 109
    see also East Asia
Six Arts, 14
Smith, D. Howard, 25, 39, 51, 54, 68
Soko, Yamaga. *See* Yamaga Soko
Song (state), 38
Song dynasty, 63, 70–71
Song-gye (Korean king), 73
Son of Heaven, 68
Sources of Chinese Tradition (Bary), 42, 49, 55, 60, 88
Sources of Japanese Tradition (Tsunoda, Bary and Keene), 74
South Korea
    democratic reform movement, 111
    modern Confucian rituals, 110
    modern influence of Confucianism, 106, 107
    women in, 108
    see also East Asia; Korea
spirits, 39
Spring and Autumn Annals, 26, 27, 50
state religious rites, 68–69
suffering, 57
Sui dynasty, 56
summer solstice, 68
Sun Yat-sen, 86–87

Taiwan, 83, 89, 106, 107, 110
    see also East Asia
Taizong (emperor), 57, 58–59
Tang dynasty
    Buddhism and Daoism in, 57, 63
    cult of Confucius, 58–61
    legends of Confucius, 60
    reemergence and growth of Confucianism, 56–58, 63
Temple of Confucius (Peking), 69
Temple of Confucius (Qufu)
    attacked during the Cultural Revolution, 90–91
    ceremonies in honor of Confucius, 70, 93
    description of, 92
    restoration of, 93
temples
    for ancestor worship, 18
    see also Confucian temples
Tiananmen Square, 99
Tokugawa Shogunate, 75–78
Turning of the Tide, The (Pas), 92

universal love, 44
Universal Soul, 57
universities, Confucian, 49–50

Vietnam
    Buddhism in, 79
    China and, 78
    Confucianism and, 63, 78–80, 96
    women in, 80
virtue
    moral education and, 42
    see also Confucian virtues
Voltaire, 77

Wang Yangming, 64
way. *See* dao; Daoism
Way of the Samurai (Yamaga Soko), 78
Western powers
    introduction of Confucianism to, 77
    relations with China, 82–85
Wheel of Life, 57
widows, 80
winter solstice, 68
women
    in Communist China, 95, 100, 108
    Confucianism and, 53, 108
    in East Asian countries, 108
    Korean Confucianism and, 75
    in Vietnam, 80
World Almanac, 9
World War II, 89
Wu Di (emperor), 49, 50
Wujing. See Five Classics
wu-wei, 58

Xinzhong Yao, 64, 108
Xunzi, 28, 42–44, 45, 46

Yamaga Soko, 78
Yen Hui (peasant), 24, 27
Yijing. See Book of Changes
yin/yang theory, 51–52
Yuan dynasty, 65
Yuan Shikai, 86

Zhongdu, 25
Zhou, duke of, 16
Zhou dynasty
    Book of History and, 16
    Confucius's life in, 12
    decline of, 42, 45
    feudalism and, 19–20
Zhu Xi
    commentaries on the Four Books, 66
    development of Neo-Confucianism and, 63, 64–65
    Korean Confucianism and, 74
    manual on ritual and decorum, 71, 75

Picture Credits

Archive Photos, 16, 38, 61, 83, 86, 90, 91
Archive Photos/Hulton Getty Collection, 10, 24, 36, 54, 67, 69, 111
Art Resource/Giraudon, 20
Art Resource/Reunion des Musees Nationaux, 65
Art Resource/Werner Forman, 70, 76, 94
CORBIS, 34, 51, 72
CORBIS/AFP, 95, 112
CORBIS/Archivo Iconographico, S.A., 43
CORBIS/Bettmann, 18, 31
CORBIS/Bohemian Nomad Picturemakers, 22
CORBIS/Pierre Colombel, 9
Digital Stock, 56
CORBIS/David and Peter Turnley, 99
CORBIS/Brian Vikander, 80
CORBIS/The Purcell Team, 14
North Wind Picture Archives, 79, 84
PhotoDisc, 101, 105

About the Author

Louise Chipley Slavicek received her master's degree in history from the University of Connecticut. Her writing credits include *Life Among the Puritans* for Lucent Books and more than thirty articles on a variety of historical subjects for scholarly journals and children's magazines. She lives in Ohio with her husband, Jim, a research biologist, and her children, Krista and Nathan.